$\mathcal{G}$REAT CHEFS COOK AT

BARBARA-JO'S

GREAT
CHEFS COOK
— AT —
BARBARA-JO'S

DISHED UP BY

Barbara-jo McIntosh

Douglas & McIntyre

VANCOUVER/TORONTO

Douglas & McIntyre
2323 Quebec Street, Suite 201
Vancouver, British Columbia
Canada v5t 4s7
www.douglas-mcintyre.com

National Library of Canada Cataloguing in Publication Data
Great chefs cook at Barbara-Jo's / dished up by Barbara-jo McIntosh.
Includes index.

ISBN 1-55365-040-9

1. Cookery. I. McIntosh, Barbara-jo.

TX714.G73 2004   645   C2003-907190-1

Editing by Lucy Kenward
Cover and interior design by Peter Cocking
Cover photographs by John Sherlock
Interior illustrations by Bernie Lyon
Printed and bound in Canada by Friesens
Printed on acid-free paper
Note: The recipes in this book are reprinted
as they appear in their original sources.

The publisher gratefully acknowledges the financial support of the
Canada Council for the Arts, the British Columbia Arts Council,
and the Government of Canada through the Book Publishing Industry
Development Program (BPIDP) for its publishing activities.

For John, who has never let me stop believing in myself, and to my mother,

for believing that Barbara-Jo's Books for Cooks was right for me

CONTENTS

FOREWORD

MY MOTHER TOLD ME that the ability to keep a secret was close to holiness. She never wavered and she never told a secret; in fact, I never knew she kept secrets because she wouldn't indicate she was party to one. But sometimes I had an inkling. . . . For instance, when my cousin was going to have a baby there was a lot of hush hush late-night phone espionage, and when we were moving from Victoria to Vancouver and I wasn't to know. Why things were kept from me remains a puzzle, but not really. I'm sure she thought I couldn't keep my mouth zipped. "But I've changed," I wailed at age fifty. . . . So the secret of what Barbara-jo was up to remained unknown to me.

The relationship between my mother, Veryl, and Barbara-jo started at Hastings Park racetrack, where my mother owned the photography concession and Barbara-jo was part of the publicity department (with food service her main focus). Barbara-jo was new to the racing business and my mother called to ask me who this young thing was and did I think she knew what she was doing. Yes, yes, I knew Barbara-jo to be first rate in all she attempted. "Alright then," said the mother, "I'll give her a chance." You see, publicity and the photography department must be in sync or the whole thing falls apart. And besides, if you don't have a lifetime of experience at the track . . . well, the whole thing might go to hell in a handcart. It is a world unto itself.

Almost overnight these two unlikelys became thick as clotted cream. Best buddies. I was only a little jealous and to add to it they had a secret.

Damn them. What could it be? The intrigue went on for months until I was driven half mad. . . .

Finally, they told me. Barbara-jo had the brilliant idea to open a cookbook store—not just any cookbook store, but one where chefs and food experts, writers and all-round epicures could get together for an evening's enlightenment and maybe a lesson. The reason for the secrecy? Not just hijackers of clever business ideas but the people who thought the concept folly were caught off guard by Ms. McIntosh's brilliance and her consequential success.

Bully for Barbara-jo . . .

VICKI GABEREAU

PREFACE

DREAMS ARE MEANT to come true. With the creation of Barbara-Jo's Books to Cooks, one of mine surely did. I've always been an avid reader and, as a young woman, I could easily imagine that I would be involved in the world of books. After working in a department store restaurant while attending high school, it was a little more difficult to envision a career in the food industry: I had no idea that carving endless slices of beef in the Marine Room at Eaton's would lead to so many wonderful opportunities in so many different forms. For thirty years, I have happily, tirelessly and wholeheartedly embraced the concept that the most important factor for a healthy earth is feeding people well.

I've always been drawn to the idea of a specialty cookbook store. But it wasn't until I read an article in *Saveur* magazine about Books for Cooks, a Notting Hill bookshop complete with a working kitchen, that I felt I could wrap body and soul around a project that would be accepted by both my community and my bankers. Looking back, I'm happy to say, the concept has been embraced with equal passion by everyone from amateur cooks to world-famous chefs.

For six years now, Barbara-Jo's Books to Cooks has been privileged to host a variety of unique culinary guests. I have always been adventuresome, and I believe that if you really want something to happen, you just have to ask. The answer could very well be yes.

I am gratified that many accomplished culinary personalities, ranging from London's *enfant terrible* Gordon Ramsay to such accomplished writers as New York's Mark Kurlansky, have responded so positively to my requests to visit the shop. British Columbia has become a very desirable destination for those interested in good food and wine, and I believe the shop has become popular for a number of reasons—including great books, warm surroundings and a dedicated staff.

This book is a natural extension of what we do at Barbara-Jo's Books to Cooks. I hope these pages capture all the joy I've felt meeting and working with so many wonderful people.

My dream could not have come true without the contribution of many special people. Besides the authors and writers I feature in this book, hundreds of other authors, celebrated chefs and purveyors have shared their secrets and philosophies with us. I thank you all. Nach Waxman, owner of New York's Kitchen Arts & Letters, has been a true mentor. I would also like to thank my small but courageous group of investors for believing that I could accomplish what I set out to do.

I am thankful for having the good sense to hire a great staff from the start. Donna Brendon, Joan Lyndon and Cath McGrath—all seasoned veterans of the book business—have greatly contributed to the success of the shop. I am grateful to my first resident chef, Frank Von Zuben, who helped me with my initial culinary program. Sylvia Molnar, Jessica Walker, Carole Smith, Lara McCormick and Tony Peneff have all left their special marks on the business.

Today, we have Ed Seliga, whose thoughtful and warm personality makes coming to work a pleasure. Adrienne O'Callaghan, my resident chef, has been with me for five years now. In that time, she's done a wonderful job at many different tasks. She cooks beautifully, teaches classes and, most importantly, makes it easy for our guest authors to be at their best.

Lastly, I'd like to thank my many faithful customers. Without their continued trust and support, I'd still be carving beef at the Marine Room.

BARBARA-JO MCINTOSH · *December 2003* · *Vancouver, BC*

THE CHEFS

⤙ ℐEFFREY ALFORD & NAOMI DUGUID ⤛

BOOK: *Hot Sour Salty Sweet*
EVENT MENU: Hot and Spicy Leaf Wraps, Buddhist Sour Soup,
Chicken and Potato Curry, Aromatic Lemongrass Patties, Issaan Salsa,
Yunnan Greens, Iced Coffee with Sweetened Condensed Milk

JEFFREY ALFORD AND HIS PARTNER and co-author, Naomi Duguid, have written four books to date. The first, *Flatbreads and Flavors,* was published before Barbara-Jo's Books to Cooks was open. The shop had the pleasure of hosting Jeffrey when *Seductions of Rice* and *Hot Sour Salty Sweet* came out. (Because they have young children, the two choose to travel separately when promoting books.) I met the cerebral Naomi over dinner in Toronto and she agreed to host an event at the shop after *Home Baking* was published. I wonder what it must be like to have four amazing books "under your skin." I say skin—as opposed to belt—because the books Jeffrey and Naomi write are an integral part of them. The life this couple has created for themselves is truly enviable.

When Jeffrey visited the shop to promote *Hot Sour Salty Sweet,* an enthusiastic crowd gathered and, of course, they left considerably more educated about the food and life of the peoples along the Mekong River. I had noticed a sadness in Jeffrey's eyes throughout the evening, but it was not until I walked him back to the hotel that I discovered his mother had died that day. To me this says everything about his love for and commitment to what he does.

In May 2001 I had lunch with Jeffrey in New York's Chinatown. We were in New York to celebrate the James Beard Foundation's annual culinary awards. *Hot Sour Salty Sweet* was nominated in two categories. I sit on the cookbook committee for the foundation and was privy to the names of the winners, but managed to divert attention from the inevitable queries. At the end of the evening, after Jeffrey and Naomi had walked away with the "gold" for cookbook of the year, he commented that I was very good at keeping secrets.

JEFFREY WRITES: From my point of view as a cookbook writer, there's only one Barbara-Jo's. When I am out on tour with a new cookbook, I am usually more or less, almost always, a little bit anxious. Either an interviewer is not going to like the book, or a cooking class is going to be a disaster, or I am going to miss an airplane, or a television host will be allergic to chilies. There is rarely anything relaxing or comfort-making about being out with a book.

Except Barbara-Jo's. I get to *sit* and watch Adrienne prepare dishes from the cookbook—far better than I do. I get to drink a glass of wine and eat food I like. And almost best of all, I know I am going to meet nice people, interesting people, and I am going to have fun. Someone in the group spent last year in Laos, another lived eight years in China and another cooks wonderfully exotic fare in a local restaurant.

I think Barbara-jo started out with a dream about how things would work. And she has made it work exactly that way.

AROMATIC LEMONGRASS PATTIES

[*mak paen*—LAOS]

½ pound boneless reasonably lean pork

(shoulder or butt, trimmed of most fat)

¼ cup sliced shallots

1 stalk lemongrass, trimmed and minced
¼ teaspoon salt
¼ teaspoon freshly ground black pepper
Makes 7 or 8 patties; serves 4 as part of a rice meal

Thinly slice the pork. Transfer to a food processor, add the shallots, lemongrass, salt, and pepper and process for about 30 seconds or until the mixture forms an even-textured ball. Turn out into a bowl. *Alternatively,* use a cleaver to finely chop the pork, first in one direction and then in the other, then fold the meat over on itself and chop again until smooth, discarding any fat or connective tissue. Add the shallots and lemongrass and continue mincing until the mixture is smooth, then transfer to a bowl.

Set out several plates. Working with wet hands, pick up a scant 2 tablespoons of the pork mixture and shape it into a flat patty 2 to 3 inches in diameter. Place on a plate and repeat with the remaining mixture; do not stack the patties. You'll have 7 or 8 patties.

Heat a large heavy skillet (or two smaller heavy skillets) over medium-high heat. Rub lightly with an oiled paper towel and add the patties. Lower the heat to medium and cook until golden on the first side, then turn over and cook for another 3 to 4 minutes, until golden and cooked through. As the patties cook, use a spatula to flatten them against the hot surface. (You can also grill or broil the patties until golden and cooked through, turning them over partway through cooking.)

Serve hot, with rice, a vegetable dish, and a salsa.

YUNNAN GREENS
[*sunni cai*—YUNNAN]
1 pound bok choi or Shanghai bok choi
(5 to 8 heads)
Salt
2 tablespoons peanut or vegetable oil
2 Thai dried red chiles
½ teaspoon minced ginger
½ cup mild vegetable broth or water
1 teaspoon cornstarch, dissolved in 2 tablespoons water
Serves 4 as one of several dishes in a meal

Place a large pot of water on to boil. Meanwhile, cut the bok choi lengthwise into thirds or quarters and place in a sink full of cold water to soak for several minutes. Wash thoroughly to get any dirt out of the base of the stalks.

When the water is boiling, add about 1 tablespoon salt, bring back to the boil, and add the bok choi. Stir with a long-handled wooden spoon to make sure all the greens are immersed. Bring back to a boil, boil for under a minute, drain, and set aside.

Heat a large wok over high heat. Add the oil and swirl to coat the wok. Toss in the chiles and ginger. Stir briefly, then add the greens and stir-fry for 30 seconds, pressing them against the sides of the wok to sear them a little. Add the broth and let it boil for about 30 seconds. Stir the cornstarch paste well, then add it together with ½ teaspoon salt. Stir-fry for another 15 to 30 seconds, turn out onto a small platter, and serve. (Warn your guests that the chiles are not for eating, just for flavour.)

⇜ COLMAN ANDREWS ⇝

BOOK: *Saveur Cooks Authentic Italian*
EVENT MENU: Bruschetta, Minestrone Genovese,
Shrimp Scampi, Pollo alla Cacciatora, Tiramisù

I FIRST MET *Saveur* magazine's Colman Andrews in his New York office. I had requested an appointment because I wanted to meet the editor behind the magazine whose article on Notting Hill's Books for Cooks inspired me to create Barbara-Jo's Books to Cooks.

Saveur has always been one of my favourite magazines. Few things make me happier than sitting in a cozy chair and reading it from beginning to end. Like many culinary magazines, *Saveur* also publishes cookbooks. *Saveur Cooks Authentic Italian* is the third in a series that combines previously published articles and recipes with new material to create a great overview of a region.

When Colman came to the shop, he seemed unconcerned with social niceties and eager to take on the task of teaching from his book. He didn't say much, preferring to fuss about in the kitchen until all the guests were assembled. Then he talked for two straight hours about the history and preparation of the recipes. Everyone in the room was completely attentive. It was as if the magazine was speaking to you.

One of the recipes Colman demonstrated that evening was the tiramisù. He adamantly advised the crowd to purchase a commercial brand of ladyfingers, explaining that the home-baked version would result in a soggy mess. Well, our Adrienne proved him wrong. She had made the perfect ladyfingers, and the tiramisù held together beautifully. Colman was impressed.

TIRAMISÙ

2 eggs, separated

½ cup sugar

½ cup mascarpone

1 cup strong, fresh, black coffee (not espresso)

12 Italian savoiardi cookies or ladyfingers

Cocoa power

Serves 4

1. Beat egg yolks with a whisk in a medium bowl. Gradually add sugar, continuing to whisk until mixture is thick, smooth, and pale yellow. Gently fold mascarpone into mixture with a rubber spatula, then set aside.

2. Put egg whites into a clean, dry mixing bowl and beat with a whisk until they form stiff but not dry peaks, fold egg whites into mascarpone mixture and set aside.

3. Pour coffee into a wide, shallow bowl. Dip 4 of the savoiardi into the coffee just long enough to moisten them without making them soggy, then arrange them side by side in a single layer on a serving platter. Spread one-third of the mascarpone mixture over the biscuits, then dust with a little cocoa powder. Repeat the entire process twice, dipping the savoiardi in coffee and layering them with mascarpone and cocoa. Refrigerate until well chilled.

✐ ELIZABETH BAIRD ➤

BOOK: *The Complete Canadian Living Cookbook*
EVENT MENU: Asparagus Miso Soup, Tomato and Mint Salad, Chutney-
Glazed Ham, Simply the Best Scalloped Potatoes, Fresh Blueberry Tart

YEARS AGO, I lived in a cottage that featured a property with a small garden.
Summer was an especially magical time. My favourite cookbook for this
short but intense season was Elizabeth Baird's *Summer Berries*. A treasured
recipe—Raspberry and Mint Pie—took full advantage of the fact that I was a
cook with backyard access to the freshest ingredients. The lingering memory
of it leaves me longing for the days when I was fortunate enough to reside in
the perfect place.

Summer Berries, originally published in 1980, is just one of many well-
known books by Elizabeth. She has continued to cook, write and appear on
television—doing whatever she can to entice us to eat well. So when Canadians talk of a "distance" between the West and Central Canada, I just mention
Elizabeth Baird. Her achievements remind all of us that we have something
in common. When Elizabeth comes to visit, the shop is full and happy.

I have chosen Elizabeth's recipe for Simply the Best Scalloped Potatoes
because my mother is constantly grousing that this recipe is not in any of her
cookery books.

SIMPLY THE BEST SCALLOPED POTATOES
6 Yukon Gold potatoes (2 lb / 1 kg)
1 small onion, sliced
SAUCE:
¼ cup (50 mL) butter
¼ cup (50 mL) all-purpose flour
1 tsp (5 mL) salt
½ tsp (2 mL) pepper
½ tsp (2 mL) dried thyme or marjoram
2½ cups (625 mL) milk
Makes 6 servings

1. Sauce: In saucepan, melt butter over medium heat. Add flour, salt, pepper and thyme; cook stirring, for 1 minute. Gradually whisk in milk; cook, whisking constantly, for 5 to 8 minutes or until boiling and thickened. Set aside.

2. Peel and thinly slice potatoes. Arrange one-third in layer in greased 8-inch (2 L) square glass baking dish or casserole; spread half of the onions over top. Repeat layers. Arrange remaining potatoes over top. Pour sauce over top.

3. Cover and bake in 350°F (180°C) oven for 1 hour. Uncover and bake for 30 minutes longer or until lightly browned and potatoes are tender. Let stand for 5 minutes before serving.

⤙ JAMES BARBER ⤚

BOOK: Many books

EVENT MENU: A collection of recipes that would fill a book

VANCOUVER CAN PROUDLY BOAST that England's James Barber has long been officially ours. James has reinvented himself a few times and—like so many of the discoveries the man has shared with us—he was way ahead of the trend when he came to the West Coast. But his best move by far was to take on the food scene in Vancouver. For thirty years now, James has written books, critiqued restaurants, been a culinary TV star and entertained the masses with his relaxed approach to food. We all have a story (or ten) to tell about him. James has entertained us at the shop on many occasions, whether teaching a class, launching a book or just popping in to browse and share his latest joke.

On one occasion James taught a children's cooking class. He was so impressed by one young lad's enthusiasm that the boy was asked to be a guest on his television show. On another evening, as he spatchcocked chickens, I witnessed a grown woman giggling and a crowd pressing their noses against the window. They all wanted to be close to the legendary "Urban Peasant." But my favourite event was the launch for the reprint of *Ginger Tea Makes Friends*. Pretty much all of the women who hold a special place in James's heart were present. We concocted a special drink for the evening and dubbed it the Gingertini. It was good.

The following is an excerpt from an article that James Barber wrote for *The Vancouver Sun:*

Barbara-jo is a bargain at best. Smart, nice warm smile, great legs, no attitude (she'll eat anything), two hours of action, takes Visa and on top of all that she'll feed you dinner and send you home with a book.

There are two kinds of foodies, those who just eat and those who also cook. Barbara-jo caters to the second, to those who want to know the how and why of what they deliver to their digestions. Her little bookshop on Mainland Street is unique, not just in Vancouver, but to my knowledge in North America. She has an enormous stock of cookbooks, new and used, first and rare editions, retro classics, all the latest and greatest and then the wine books, the food books, the myth, mythology, history and exotic how-to's like kosher-style wine-braised vegetarian unicorns, if that's what you need.

But it's not just the books that drag in the johns. She has a full-sized operating kitchen slap in the middle of the store—a real Mercedes of a kitchen, and it works. The store smells of Rob Feenie and Donna Hay and Thailand and cookies and roast chicken—three deep breaths and every brain cell stops working, except for the food receptors (those primitive ones we inherited from dogs). Something gets cooked in there most every day, either by touring cookbook authors or Adrienne, the resident chef.

GINGERTINIS

Make a strong syrup by simmering copious amounts of grated ginger in water. In a martini shaker place ice, 3 parts vodka to 1 part syrup and shake. Pour into chilled martini glasses and serve with wedge of lemon.

⤙ *J*OHN BISHOP ⤚

BOOK: *Simply Bishop's*

EVENT MENU: Asian Tuna Tartare with Scallion Pancakes,
Smoked Salmon and Cucumber with Pickled Ginger,
Roasted Pear and Goat Cheese Phyllo Pastries, Pesto-crusted Halibut with
Red Lentil Dahl, Roasted Butternut Squash with Maple-thyme Butter,
Belgian Chocolate Soufflés with Crème Anglaise

DOUG HAGER, who doubles as both my lawyer and a valued customer, has advised me that my life would be a lot easier if I could arrange for John Bishop to come in and teach a class once a week. He may have a point. John is truly loved in this city. So much so that I could almost charge for standing room when he holds court at the shop.

I first met John Bishop when we both worked for Umberto Menghi. I was at Al Porto in Gastown and John was at Umberto's Yellow House. Many people still have fond memories of John's warm and caring manner during his time there. In 1984, John left Umberto to open Bishop's, a tony restaurant on Vancouver's west side that maintains John's traditional concern for his patrons. I find it very comforting to know that I can walk into Bishop's today and recapture the warmth that comes with feeling you are truly welcome.

Simply Bishop's is John's third cookbook—and my favourite. An evolved chef, John now cooks with organic products in season. For those of us who remember John from his days at the Yellow House, the book's combination of pure ingredients served with love and respect is classic John Bishop.

PESTO-CRUSTED HALIBUT WITH
RED LENTIL DAHL

DAHL:

2 Tbsp. (30 mL) vegetable oil
1 small onion, ¼-inch/6-mm dice
2 garlic cloves, crushed
1 Tbsp. (15 mL) grated fresh ginger

1 cup (250 mL) red lentils

½ tsp. (2.5 mL) garam masala

½ tsp. (2.5 mL) cumin

½ tsp. (2.5 mL) turmeric

4 cups (1 L) water

½ tsp. (2.5 mL) sugar

½ tsp. (2.5 mL) salt

Freshly ground black pepper

PESTO:

½ lb. (250 g) fresh basil leaves

4 garlic cloves

2 Tbsp. (30 mL) toasted pine nuts

Pinch of coarse salt

½ cup (125 mL) grated Parmesan cheese

½ cup (125 mL) extra-virgin olive oil

HALIBUT:

4 halibut fillets (each 6 oz. / 170 g)

Salt and freshly ground black pepper

4 servings

TO MAKE DAHL: Heat vegetable oil in a large saucepan on medium heat. Sauté onion, garlic and ginger until onion is soft, 4 to 5 minutes. Add lentils, garam masala, cumin and turmeric. (If you like your dahl a little spicier, add a dried whole chili pepper or two, then remove at the end of the cooking process.) Add water and bring to a simmer on medium-high heat, skimming off any foam that appears on the surface. Add sugar, salt and pepper. Cover and simmer for 45 minutes. (Lentil dahl can made ahead and will keep for 1 to 2 days in the refrigerator.)

TO MAKE PESTO: Place basil, garlic, pine nuts, coarse salt and Parmesan cheese in a blender or food processor and grind into a paste. Slowly add extra-virgin olive oil until smooth. Refrigerate until needed. (Any extra pesto will keep for a week refrigerated, 3 months frozen.)

TO MAKE HALIBUT: Preheat the oven to 400°F/200°C and line a baking sheet with parchment paper. Take 1 Tbsp./15 mL of pesto for each halibut fillet and rub in, then place fish on the prepared baking sheet. Bake until just cooked through so that flesh is opaque and firm to the touch, about 10 minutes.

To serve, reheat dahl and spoon onto warmed plates. Top each with a piece of halibut.

~ MARK BITTMAN ~

BOOK: *The Minimalist Cooks Dinner*
EVENT MENU: Spanish-Style Shrimp, Pasta alla Gricia,
Fastest Roast Chicken, Glazed Carrots, Sautéed Shiitake Mushrooms,
Dried Fruit Poached in Port

MARK BITTMAN HAS BEEN to the shop on so many occasions that I've actually lost count, but his first visit, on November 9, 1998, holds a special place in my heart. I'd organized a signing at the shop, even though Mark's visit to Vancouver was to be a short one. I wanted to meet him as I had a natural affinity for *Fish*, an earlier publication. In addition, his newly published book, *How to Cook Everything*, chronicled an immense culinary journey via the home kitchen. The real attraction, however, was his column "The Minimalist," featured every Wednesday in *The New York Times*. This column, influenced by both regional and global ingredients, features quick, snappy ideas and improvisations for recipes that make preparing today's dinner effortless.

Mark had appeared on the Gabereau show earlier that day and was flying off to Winnipeg later that afternoon. About 2 PM, sporting a poppy, he swaggered into the shop announcing his pleasure at our city's commitment to remembering November 11. (Apparently, the United States doesn't share the tradition of wearing poppies to honour veterans.) I was delighted and amused with this born and bred New Yorker.

The signing went well. Mark was impressed and expressed a desire to return. Consequent visits have included excursions ranging from mushroom foraging to Bard on the Beach, not to mention some highly enjoyable lessons on how to eat everything at a selection of fine local restaurants.

We now stock many of Mark's books, including *The Minimalist Cooks at Home*, *The Minimalist Cooks Dinner* and *The Minimalist Entertains*. They all sell very well.

MARK WRITES: Barbara-Jo's Books to Cooks is not only my favourite cookbook shop in North America, it's my favourite place for cooking classes and demonstrations. And for meeting the people who actually buy and use my books. It is an intensely personal place, independent and just about as far away from the corporate book world as you can get. (It's also a place where you find food-related books you do not see elsewhere.) Part of this, of course, is because it's owned and run by Barbara-jo McIntosh. Barbara-jo is usually in the shop, but even if she is not, the place is filled with her warm, welcoming and intelligent spirit. There is a love here, not only of cookbooks, but also of books in general, of cookbooks as literature, of the world of food and its gentler, slower—more leisurely and nourishing, as opposed to nutritional—side.

PASTA ALLA GRICIA

TIME: 30 minutes

2 tablespoons extra virgin olive oil

½ cup minced guanciale, pancetta, or bacon (about ¼ pound)

Salt

1 pound linguine or another long pasta

½ cup grated Pecorino, Romano, or more to taste

Freshly ground black pepper

Makes 3 main-course to 6 first-course servings

1. Begin heating water for the pasta. In a small saucepan, combine the oil and meat and turn the heat to medium. Cook, stirring occasionally, until the meat is nicely browned, about 10 minutes. Turn off the heat.

2. Salt the boiling pasta water and cook the pasta until it is tender but not mushy. Before draining the pasta, remove about a cup of the cooking water and reserve it.

3. Toss the drained pasta with the meat; its juices and stir in the cheese. If the mixture is dry, add a little of the pasta cooking water (or a little olive oil). Toss in lots of the black pepper and serve.

FASTEST ROAST CHICKEN

TIME: 45 to 60 minutes

1 whole chicken (3 to 4 pounds)

Salt and freshly ground black pepper

Makes 4 servings

1. Preheat the oven to 450°F. Five minutes after turning on the oven, place a cast-iron or other heavy, ovenproof skillet on a rack set low in the oven. (Alternatively, put the skillet over high heat about 3 minutes before the oven is hot.) Season the chicken with salt and pepper.

2. When the oven is hot, about 10 minutes later, carefully place the chicken, breast side up, in the hot skillet. Roast, undisturbed, for 30 minutes, or until

an instant-read thermometer inserted in the meaty part of the thigh registers 155°F. Remove from the oven, let rest for a minute or two, then carve and serve.

Bob Blumer

BOOK: *Off the Eaten Path*

EVENT MENU: Shrimp "on the Bar-b," Pepper-crusted Maple Glazed Salmon, (I can't believe it's not) Creamed Corn, Grilled Asparagus Spears, Pound Cake "Fries" with Raspberry "Catsup"

SOMETIMES, WHEN I RECEIVE a request for an author to come visit, I just have to giggle. Such was the case when the call came explaining that Bob Blumer and his Toastermobile—an Airstream trailer with a fully equipped kitchen and an exterior that features two giant pieces of popped-up toast—were planning to finish their North American tour in Vancouver. Bob Blumer (a.k.a. the Surreal Gourmet) is a wiry, energetic man with a hairdo that makes him look as if he's just stuck his finger in an electric socket. He's not afraid to push life to the limit. So when Bob writes a cookbook, be prepared for anything—including really tasty food delivered with a truly unusual spin.

Although Adrienne may grouse about the corn on the cob she was asked to peel and scrape, the toughest part of organizing Bob's event was making room for the Toastermobile outside the store. We had to get a permit from the city to block off a few hundred feet of Mainland Street on a Saturday night. However, the meal Bob cooked in his trailer—and ultimately presented to us in the shop—was adorably eccentric and delivered with aplomb.

BOB WRITES: Vancouver, August 12, 1999: I am as greasy as a pig from cooking dinner all night in the sweltering summer heat. Just like a real toaster, my larger-than-life version is red hot on the inside. With the oven cranked to 500 degrees, the gas range fired up and no air conditioning, it is hot enough in here to roast me alive, right along with the pepper-crusted maple glazed salmon and purple potatoes I just finished serving to eighteen guests in Barbara-jo's cookbook store.

About three nights a week, the crew and I become a mobile dinner party commando squad. We roll up to a pre-arranged venue, pop out the pass-through window on the Toastermobile and start serving appetizers faster than most people can microwave a burrito. The controlled frenzy of chopping, slicing, grating, grilling, whisking, cooking, plating and serving that follows has the intensity of an emergency room during a full moon.

The day, which started in the distant haze of a 7 AM TV appearance, is almost done. Any non-cooking time I spent on my celery phone, doing interviews, pinning down scheduling details, juggling sponsor requests, finalizing

details of media appearances, arranging drop shipments of supplies and saving the country—one palate at a time—from the evils of mediocre food. I'll nap when I'm dead—that is, if this tour doesn't kill me first.

Suddenly, my sous-chef and I are drawn by the wailing guitar of a vintage David Bowie CD and spontaneously we start bouncing around the Toastermobile—all the manic intensity of the day pouring out as pure motion energy. Guests trickling out from Barbara-Jo's gaze in astonishment at the sight of two sweat-drenched, food-stained chefs in a Toastermobile, rockin' to the music, oblivious to the Yaletown surroundings.

(I CAN'T BELIEVE IT'S NOT) CREAMED CORN

8 ears of corn, *husked*
2 tablespoons butter (optional)
¼ teaspoon chipotle chili powder (optional)
Salt and freshly ground pepper to taste
Serves 4

1. Using a sharp paring knife, start at the top of the cob and score the middle of each row of kernels. The object here is to puncture the individual casings so that it is easier to force out the contents (as described in step 2). The depth of the incision, as well as your ability to slice a straight line, is of no consequence.
2. Grab your largest pot and a common dinner knife. Hold the cob inside the pot. Starting at the top of the cob, run the back side of the blade down the cob, using pressure to force out the meat and milk from the casings. Be forewarned, this is a messy job (hence the pot) that requires a healthy amount of muscle power. If possible, do this outdoors.
3. Discard the cobs and transfer the corn mash to a smaller pot. If you decide to add butter and chipotle, do it here. Warm over medium heat for a few watchful minutes, stirring frequently. If you warm corn for too long, or over too high a temperature, the natural liquids will evaporate and the corn will become gooey.
4. Season with salt and pepper, and serve immediately.

◄ *T*ISH BOYLE ➤

BOOK: *The Good Cookie*

EVENT MENU: Brandied Eggnog Cookies, Amy-oes, Almond Raspberry
Tea Cakes, Triple-Ginger Pecan Biscotti

SATURDAY AND SUNDAY AFTERNOONS we have a number of regular patrons
who gather round the shop just to see what kind of cookie there is to be sam-
pled. (I don't think Donna would work on Sundays if she didn't have a plate
of cookies to pass.) So when Tish Boyle published *The Good Cookie*, we
knew the book would become the object of Adrienne's desire when choosing
what cookie to bake for weekenders.

We decided we should hold two events when Tish came to visit, one for
the children and another for the grown-up cookie lovers. Unfortunately, Tish
came to us feeling rather poorly and we did not see her perform at her best.
But the recipes and results were magnificent—the book is brilliant—and Tish
could not believe how well behaved the children (and their parents) were.

BRANDIED EGGNOG COOKIES

EGGNOG COOKIES:

1 cup (2 sticks) unsalted butter, softened

½ cup granulated sugar

1 large egg yolk

1 teaspoon vanilla extract

¼ teaspoon freshly grated nutmeg

⅛ teaspoon salt

2 cups all-purpose flour

Coarse sugar for sprinkling

BRANDY CREAM FILLING:

3 tablespoons unsalted butter, softened

1 cup plus 2 tablespoons confectioners' sugar

1 tablespoon brandy

1 teaspoon vanilla extract

GARNISH:

Freshly grated nutmeg

SPECIAL EQUIPMENT:

1½-inch fluted square or round cookie cutter

½-inch aspic cutter (of any shape)

or ½-inch plain pastry tip (such as Ateca #6)

Makes 30 sandwich cookies

MAKE THE DOUGH

1. In the bowl of an electric mixer, using the paddle attachment, beat the butter and sugar at medium speed until combined, about 1 minute. Add the egg yolk, vanilla extract, nutmeg, and salt and mix until combined, scraping down the sides of the bowl as necessary. At low speed, add the flour and mix until combined. Turn the dough out onto a piece of plastic wrap, pat it into a rectangle, and wrap it up. Refrigerated for at least 1 hour, until firm (or up to 3 days).

CUT AND BAKE THE COOKIES

2. Position a rack in the center of the oven and preheat the oven to 350°F. Line two baking sheets with parchment paper or foil.

3. Place the chilled dough on a lightly floured work surface and sprinkle it lightly with flour. Using a rolling pin, roll the dough out to a thickness of ⅛ inch. Using a 1½-inch fluted square or round cookie cutter, cut out as many cookies as possible from the dough. Using a ½-inch aspic cutter (of any shape) or ½-inch plain pastry tip, cut out the centers of half of the cookies (these will be the tops). Stack and press together the scraps and chill for 15 minutes before rerolling. Carefully transfer the cookies to the prepared baking sheets, placing the tops and bottoms on separate sheets (the tops will take a minute or so less to bake than the bottoms). Sprinkle the cookies with coarse sugar. Bake the cookies, one sheet at a time, for 9 to 11 minutes, or until lightly browned on the bottom (not on top). Transfer the cookies to wire racks and cool completely.

MAKE THE FILLING

4. In the bowl of an electric mixer, using the paddle attachment, beat the butter at medium speed until creamy, about 30 seconds. Gradually add the confectioners' sugar, brandy, and vanilla extract and beat until blended. Scrape down the sides of the bowl. Increase the speed to high and beat until the filling is creamy, about 2 minutes.

ASSEMBLE THE COOKIES

5. Spread about ¼ teaspoon of the filling onto the bottom of one of the whole cookies. Top with one of the cut-out cookies, right side up, and press the cookies lightly together. Repeat with the remaining cookies and filling. Grate a bit of nutmeg on top of each cookie. Serve the cookies at room temperature or chilled.

Store in an airtight container at room temperature for 3 days or refrigerated for up to a week.

⭇ FRIEND OF THE SHOP: ⭌
ROBBIE BURNS

Had my shop been alive when poet Robbie Burns was,
I believe he would have stopped by.

IF YOU BELIEVE IN SPIRITS—and Robbie Burns surely did—you'll definitely feel that Robbie's spirit is in the house on January 25. Every year on this day, we host a Scotch nosing at the shop to celebrate Robbie's birth.

Robert Burns was a man who cared passionately about all the things life had to offer. We know of his magnificent prose, his affection for the bottle and his many affairs of the heart. But what is not widely known is that he had a fierce desire to change his world, one that supported racism as a means for money and power. He really did love humankind. So every year I take great pleasure in honouring this man. His poetry makes me cry and I am happy that a man's work (for a' that) is capable o' that.

Two men—Daryl Prefontaine and Bruce MacKenzie—have led the nosings in alternate years. Each of them has presented a strong case for imbibing fine scotch. (Not that those who attend need a great deal of convincing.) They continually manage to entertain us with some undiscovered fact, blend or method that pertains to this liquid gold.

Of course, the evening would not be complete without a sampling of haggis, a piper to bring it in and a well-spoken gentleman to address this Scottish delicacy by way of Robbie's famous ode.

Here is the last verse of "Address to a Haggis" by Robert Burns, written in 1786:

> *Ye Pow'rs, wha mak mankind your care,*
> *And dish them out their bill o' fare,*
> *Auld Scotland wants nae skinking ware*
> *That jaups in luggies;*
> *But, if you wish her gratefu' prayer*
> *Gie her a haggis!*

The following is a list of books we have used as guides for these events:
Complete Guide to Single Malt Scotch (third and fourth editions),
    by Michael Jackson
Malt Whisky, by Charles MacLean
Scotland and Its Whiskies, by Michael Jackson
Whisky: The Water of Life—Uisge Beatha, by Helen Arthur

⤝ 𝒻RIEND OF THE SHOP: ⤞
CHRISTINA BURRIDGE

Christina Burridge is a wine writer
who spends much time educating herself about wine.

CHRISTINA BURRIDGE WRITES: Reading about wine is sometimes better than drinking it. More than a creative act, it's re-creative: the right words can not only bring back but also improve past experiences. Good wine writers stimulate both memory and anticipation.

My father gave me my first wine book when I was a teenager, during an era in which most of the wine we drank was homemade dandelion. I can still remember the thrill of reading about such romantic names as Gevrey-Chambertin, Vosne-Romanée and Nuits-St.-Georges and the anticipation of one day swirling those lovely descriptions around in my mouth. To this day I can call up every detail of the occasion, my birthday: my father's enthusiasm, and the two of us reading the book together.

I still have that book, a wine atlas now hopelessly out of date, along with many others that have spilled out of the overflowing bookshelves and onto the floor. Some volumes I am given, most of them I buy, nearly always with the same eager excitement that accompanied that first book. And I buy them all—reference books, personal histories, autobiographies (which are always so much more revealing than posthumous biographies) and books about all the journeys that wine has led people to. Like wine, some of these stories age well, some really aren't much to start with and some are truly exceptional.

Wine books are much more than just information (I can get that over the Internet or even on my Palm Pilot), they are companions that mark my own journey. And they come with one other great advantage—bookstores. Barbara-jo's shop is a cellar of anticipation. With all the different worlds of food and wine lining the shelves and oftentimes the smell of food cooking on the stove, there is always a sense of choice, of the future. For me, being in the shop evokes journeys to plan and to remember, feasts and love affairs, sad days and joyous ones, cheer and consolation both on the page and in the glass.

⟞ $\mathscr{D}$IANE CLEMENT ⟝

BOOK: *Zest for Life*

EVENT MENU: James Beard's Crudités, Circa 1974,
Flaming Spinach Salad, Christian's Seared Scallops with Madras Curry
Sauce and Corn Pudding, Starllies Almond Cake

THE DESCRIPTION that comes to mind when I think of Diane Clement is "whirlwind diva." Just how much energy can one glamorous woman have? In Madame's case, a lot. Spend a few moments with Diane and you'll be amazed at her spirit. Spend a few hours and you'll feel humbled.

Diane began writing cookbooks in the seventies. Somewhere I have tucked away her labours of love, *The Gourmet Eight* 1 and 2. They are hand-typed, spiral-bound collections of recipes compiled by a group of women who enjoyed cooking together. Then came the multi-volume Chef on the Run series and *Diane Clement at the Tomato*. *Zest for Life* is a memoir as much as it is a cookbook, chronicling her celebrated life through the recipes she has created, borrowed and shared with hundreds of Canadians from coast to coast.

Diane has been to the shop on many occasions. She is always cheerful, positive and ready to entertain. When Diane asked if she could film her television spots in the shop, I was eager to comply. She liked to tape seven spots at a go, ensuring that a grand assembly of guests would gather for an afternoon of conviviality. As always, she was the perfect host.

For one of these visits, Diane asked me to cook a recipe with her. I chose the Fried Salmon and Corn Fritters. Well, the hot oil started to pop—all over us. We didn't know whether to cry from the pain or laugh because the whole thing seemed so silly. The camera kept rolling and the hilarious incident made it to air.

Diane is now semi-retired from her responsibilities to the food world but is still fully committed to a life of joy.

Diane prepared the following recipe for Margaret Trudeau when she appeared on Margaret's television show in the 1980s.

FLAMING SPINACH SALAD

3 bags (10-oz size) fresh spinach

1 lb bacon

2 oz brandy

3 hard boiled eggs

Sunflower seeds, toasted

DRESSING:

⅓ cup red wine vinegar

Juice of 1 lemon

¼ cup granulated sugar

½ tsp Worcestershire sauce

¼ to ½ tsp Dijon mustard, to taste

Serves 6 to 8

METHOD: Remove stems from the spinach, wash and dry well and store in sealed plastic bags in the refrigerator until ready to serve (will keep fresh for two or three days). Fry the bacon until crisp; drain well, reserving the fat. Chop the bacon into small squares and refrigerate. Prepare dressing.

DRESSING: Whisk the first five dressing ingredients, then add the ¾ cup bacon fat and blend well. Refrigerate until ready to serve.

Just before serving, break the spinach leaves into bite-sized pieces and divide among 6 to 8 salad bowls. Mix the dressing in a skillet with the chopped bacon and heat until very hot. Pour into a chafing dish to bring to the table and keep hot over a candle. Heat the brandy in a small saucepan until it begins to vapourize, then pour it very slowly over the hot dressing and set it alight. Pour about 3 tbsp of the flaming dressing over each salad, and decorate with slices of egg and toasted sunflower seeds.

PREPARATION TIME: 25 minutes

⟨ REGAN DALEY ⟩

BOOK: *In the Sweet Kitchen*
EVENT MENU: Cazuela Pie, Valrhona Molten Chocolate Cakes
with an Espresso Crème Anglaise, à la Avalon,
Quince and Brioche Bread Pudding with Dried Sour Cherries

WE HAVE A NUMBER of memorable gentlemen who frequent the shop. But one in particular—Rhys Davies—has shown a genuine verve for baking. I have never seen him more animated than the evening that Regan Daley held court in our kitchen. But then, he had every reason to be excited. Regan is a bright and talented young woman whose baking skills are inspirational.

I often refer to the science of baking as "the other side of the kitchen" because, unlike some other culinary abilities, it demands a firm and precise hand that leaves little room for the pleasures of intuition. The side of the kitchen that I am most comfortable in tends to stereotype bakers as overly precise.

Regan doesn't fit this stereotype. Although she believes strongly in certain principles (including the importance of exact measurement and the use of pure ingredients), her relaxed approach to baking is both fun and infectious. Just ask Rhys Davies. Rhys was so inspired by Regan's methods that he made a beautiful wedding cake for his son.

Regan did not prepare this cake the evening she was with us, but I love making this recipe using local British Columbia hazelnuts so much that I have snuck it into this book.

TOASTED HAZELNUT POUND CAKE
1½ cups hazelnuts, toasted and skinned
(see book for tips)
1 cup granulated sugar
1 cup unsalted butter, at room temperature
½ cup tightly packed light brown sugar
4 large eggs, at room temperature

2 teaspoons pure vanilla extract

2 cups all purpose flour

2½ teaspoons baking powder

½ teaspoon salt

½ cup whipping cream (35%)

1 tablespoon pure hazelnut oil, optional,

but highly recommended!

Additional unsalted butter, at room temperature,

for greasing the pan

Serves 10 to 12

1. Preheat the oven to 350°. Butter and lightly flour a 9-inch springform pan and set aside. In a food processor, pulse the toasted hazelnuts with 2 table-spoons of the granulated sugar until finely ground. Take care not to over-grind the hazelnuts to the point where they become a nut butter, or the cake will be oily and heavy. Set the nut mixture aside.

2. In the bowl of an electric mixer fitted with the paddle attachment, or a large mixing bow with a wooden spoon, cream the butter until light, then add the white and brown sugars and cream the mixture until it is light, pale and fluffy. Add the eggs, one at a time, beating well after each addition and scraping down the sides of the bowl periodically. Don't worry if the mixture looks separated and broken; it will come together perfectly when the flour is incorporated. Beat in the vanilla.

3. Sift the flour, baking powder and salt together, then stir in the nut mixture. Add this to the butter mixture in three additions, alternating with the cream in two additions, beginning and ending with the dry ingredients. Mix only enough to mostly incorporate each addition, and if you are using a mixer, switch to a rubber spatula or flat wooden spoon for the last addition of flour. Add the hazelnut oil with the last addition of cream. As soon as the dry ingredients are completely moistened, scrape the batter into the prepared pan and place the pan in the centre of the oven.

4. Bake for 1 hour and 10 minutes to 1 hour and 20 minutes, or until the top

springs back when lightly touched, the sides are just beginning to pull away from the pan and a wooden skewer inserted in the centre of the cake comes out clean. Transfer the pan to a wire rack and cool 20 to 30 minutes. Run a thin-bladed knife around the outside of the cake, then remove the sides of the pan. Cool the cake on the rack completely before serving or wrapping and storing. This cake is actually better the second day, stored well wrapped at room temperature, and can be kept for up to 5 days, stored in the refrigerator. Either way, it needs absolutely no accompaniment, not even a dusting of icing sugar.

⤛ 𝒯OM DOUGLAS ⤜

BOOK: *Tom Douglas' Seattle Kitchen*
EVENT MENU: Smoky Eggplant with Seed Bread, Palace Olive
Poppers, Lobster and Shiitake Potstickers with Sake Sauce,
Etta's Pit-roasted Salmon with Grilled Shiitake Relish and Cornbread
Pudding, Dahlia Pear Tart with Caramel Sauce

TOM DOUGLAS HIMSELF! Yes indeed, the owner of not one but four great eateries in Seattle. The cover of Tom's first book, *Tom Douglas' Seattle Kitchen,* features a larger-than-life lumberjack figure holding a very big salmon. I believe this is an image many people have of men born and bred in the Pacific Northwest. So, yes, though Tom is from elsewhere, he fits the stereotype. And the book is a special tribute to the city he now calls home.

Much more than a cookbook, *Seattle Kitchen* is a food lover's guide to getting along and eating well in this coastal town. At the shop, a sold-out audience watched this teddy bear of a man cook a lot, growl a little and share his love for food. Tom had contracted food poisoning earlier that day, but it did not detract from a stellar performance and a great meal. The crowd left happy.

SMOKY EGGPLANT WITH SEED BREAD

2 globe eggplants

(weighing about 1½ pounds each)

½ onion, sliced into ⅓-inch-thick rings

⅓-cup extra virgin olive oil, plus more for grilling

Kosher salt and freshly ground black pepper

1 tablespoon chopped garlic

3 tablespoons tahini

2 tablespoons fresh lemon juice

1 tablespoon chopped fresh flat-leaf parsley

Seed Bread (recipe follows)

Makes 6 to 8 servings

1. Fire up the grill or preheat the broiler. Poke the eggplants with a fork (to keep them from exploding) and grill or broil on a baking sheet until blackened on all sides and very soft, 20 to 30 minutes. Brush the onions lightly with olive oil, sprinkle with salt and pepper, and grill (or broil) then until softened, 7 to 10 minutes. Allow the eggplants to cool enough to handle them, then cut them in half lengthwise and scoop out the pulp with a large spoon. Discard the skins. Chop the pulp and place in a bowl (you should have about 2½ cups chopped eggplant). Finely chop the grilled onions and add to the eggplant. Set aside.

2. Heat the ⅓-cup olive oil in a small skillet over medium heat. Add the chopped garlic and cook gently, stirring, for a few minutes. Remove the skillet from the heat and allow to cool slightly, then add the garlic to the eggplant-onion mixture. In a small bowl, mix the tahini and lemon juice together, then add to the eggplant-onion mixture. Add the chopped parsley and mix well. Season to taste with salt and pepper.

   ON THE PLATE: Serve the eggplant in a wide, shallow bowl drizzled with extra virgin olive oil and accompanied by olives and warm seed bread or pita.

   IN THE GLASS: Try a Demestica red from Greece or a light Zinfandel.

SEED BREAD

4 cups all-purpose flour

2 tablespoons sesame seeds

1 tablespoon poppy seeds

2 teaspoons fennel seeds

2 teaspoons kosher salt

1½ teaspoons baking powder

½ teaspoon freshly ground black pepper

1⅓ cups water

¾ cup olive oil

Makes 8 flatbreads; 6 to 8 servings

1. In a bowl, combine the flour, seeds, salt, baking powder, and pepper. Add the water and ¼ cup of the olive oil and mix by hand until a dough is formed. Knead the dough for 3 to 4 minutes. Place the dough in a bowl, cover with plastic wrap, and allow to rest for half an hour.

2. Preheat the oven to 400°F. Remove the dough from the bowl and divide it into 8 pieces. With a lightly floured rolling pin, roll each piece into a 6-inch round about ⅛ inch thick on a lightly floured work surface.

3. For each flatbread, heat 1 tablespoon of the remaining olive oil in a skillet over medium-high heat, then panfry the flatbread until golden brown, about one minute, flip, and place in the oven until the other side is golden and the bread is cooked through, about 2 more minutes. Repeat for the remaining flatbreads.

⤚ JILL DUPLEIX ⤙

BOOK: *Simple Food*

EVENT MENU: Tuna and White Bean Toast,
Grilled Zucchini Salad, Little Egg and Ham Pies, Roasted
Pesto Chicken, Crash Hot Potatoes, Mediterranean Vegetables,
Espresso Prunes with Caramel Yogurt

JILL DUPLEIX is a native and citizen of Australia. But when we met she was living in London, England. At the time she and husband Terry Durack had decided to spend four years working there—Jill taking the position of "Sunday Cook" for the London *Times,* and Terry becoming restaurant critic for the *Independent.* Jill came to Vancouver to promote the release of *Simple Food,* a book that clearly supports the life the couple shares through their mutual passion for food.

Jill and Terry, like many Australians, have always been fond of travel, and one of the reasons for moving to London was the central location of the city. Every weekend (with the help of Ryanair's cheap fares) Jill and Terry could fly efficiently to any number of exotic destinations. These trips, along with Jill's natural curiosity for intense flavour combinations, have inspired *Simple Food.* A deliciously worldly collection of recipes, *Simple Food* is a cookery book that cleverly employs familiar ingredients and simple techniques.

Jill enchanted the group that gathered to meet her that spring evening. Yes, her recipes were wonderful, everything the book promised, and she shared so much with us—including a love for her husband and their life together. I was left feeling that this woman is more than well fed.

LITTLE EGG AND HAM PIES
1 tsp olive oil or butter
12 thin slices good-quality ham
12 extra-large free-range eggs
2 tbsp cream
Sea salt
Freshly ground black pepper
2 tbsp roughly chopped parsley
4 tbsp grated parmesan
Makes 12

Heat the oven to 350°F. Lightly oil or butter a 12-hole muffin pan. Line the bottom and most of the sides of each cup with a slice of ham, then break an egg into the hollow. Drizzle with the cream and scatter with sea salt, pepper, parsley, and parmesan.

Bake for 15 to 20 minutes until the egg is just set and starting to shrink away from the sides of the cup. Leave to cool for 5 minutes, then run a knife around each cup to loosen the ham and egg, and remove to a wire rack. Eat warm, or at room temperature.

⤙ *R* OB FEENIE ⤚

BOOK: *Rob Feenie Cooks at Lumière*
EVENT MENU: Scallop Carpaccio with Jalapeño, Mint and
Cilantro, Tuna Tartare with Tamari Vinaigrette,
Sake and Maple Marinated Sablefish with a Citrus and Soy Sauce,
Walnut Cake with Maple Ice Cream

IT GIVES ME great pleasure to note that Rob Feenie and I both graduated from Dubrulle Culinary School. That said, I confess that there's a grand gap between our cooking abilities. My impetus to take a six-month intensive course behind the stove was to understand the workings of a commercial kitchen—to know and feel what a chef must do to run a successful operation. Rob had a different motivation. He was determined to become a world famous master chef. Today, this homegrown lad (who once considered becoming a fireman) is an international culinary king.

When people ask me what makes Rob Feenie special, I reply: "Rob has two cookbooks, two restaurants and a national television show. Not to mention knowing just about everybody there is to know in the world of high-end cookery." It takes a particular type of personality to achieve all this, and an intense focus that doesn't always make for an easy personal or professional life. But when Rob performs at the shop, the crowds throng. And when I eat his food, I have sweet dreams.

TUNA TARTARE WITH TAMARI VINAIGRETTE

1 lb. sushi-grade ahi or big-eye tuna

TAMARI VINAIGRETTE:

⅓ cup orange juice

⅓ cup rice vinegar

2 Tbsp. tamari

1 Tbsp. ponzu sauce (available in Asian stores)

or 1 Tbsp. equal parts tamari, lemon juice and mirin

¼ cup sesame oil

1 Tbsp. fresh cilantro, finely shredded

1 tsp. toasted black sesame seeds

2 tsp. finely chopped green onion

1 tomato peeled, seeded and cut into ¼-inch dice

2 Tbsp. shredded nori

1 avocado

¼ lemon

1 Tbsp. tobiko (flying fish roe) for garnish

mixed baby greens tossed with lemon oil

for garnish (see book for details)

Cilantro oil for garnish (see book for details)

Tamari reduction for garnish (optional)

(see book for details)

Serves 4

Cut the tuna into a very small dice, approximately ¼ inch. Dicing the fish into small pieces is easier when the fish is chilled.

For the vinaigrette, combine orange juice, vinegar, tamari and ponzu sauce. Gradually whisk in sesame oil until emulsified. Keep refrigerated until ready to use.

In a mixing bowl, just before you are ready to serve, combine tuna, cilantro, black sesame seeds, green onion and tomato. Add 4 Tbsp. tamari vinaigrette and mix gently. Season with salt and freshly ground black pepper. Taste and adjust seasonings. Add shredded nori and keep refrigerated until ready to use. Taste again before serving and add a little lemon juice, if necessary.

Before serving, peel, seed and dice avocado. Gently mix with lemon juice.

To serve, place some avocado in the middle of plates, using a cookie cutter or round mold as a guide. Place tuna tartare on top. Sprinkle with a little tobiko. Top with mixed greens. Drizzle cilantro oil and tamari reduction around tartare and remove mold. Serve immediately.

❮ *G*ALE GAND ❯

BOOK: *Gale Gand's Just a Bite*
EVENT MENU: Fudge Tartlets with Peanut Butter Ice Cream
and Cabernet Caramel, Chocolate Pots-de-crème with Orange Whipped
Cream, French Macaroons with Coffee Cream

IN THE SAME WAY I refer to François Payard as the Pastry King of New York, I feel compelled to crown Gale Gand the Pastry Queen of Chicago. I felt this way before the James Beard Foundation made her true culinary royalty in 2001—honouring her with its Outstanding Pastry Chef Award—and she became Pastry Queen of the entire United States.

Gale came to us in the fall of 2000 when *Gale Gand's Just a Bite*, her second solo cookbook, was published. We have a group of pastry ladies-in-waiting who regularly visit the shop and they all came to pay their respects to Madame.

Gale is co-owner of Tru Restaurant in Chicago, with her ex-husband Rick Tramonto. Rick is the executive chef and Gale, of course, rules the sweet kitchen. The restaurant is justly celebrated for its unique approach. To quote Gale on the tradition of giving each departing guest a custom-made lollipop, "It is most satisfying to observe the most conservative of business

people strolling through the streets of Chicago licking a Tru lollipop." Over the years, Gale has made thousands of them.

That's not the only tradition Gale has started. She is also responsible for what you might call "the tiara tradition." It is a custom of the James Beard Foundation that the previous year's recipient of an award passes it on to the new winner. In May 2002, Gale sparkled as she came to the stage and donned a tiara. Soon after, there were screams, tears and much joy as Gale placed the tiara on the head of a new queen, Spago's Sherry Yard.

FUDGE TARTLETS WITH PEANUT BUTTER ICE CREAM AND CABERNET CARAMEL

You will need: an ice-water bath (see book for details),
an ice cream machine, at least 2 mini-muffin
tins, about 24 cups each, nonstick cooking spray

FOR THE ICE CREAM:

1 quart (4 cups) half-and-half

½ vanilla bean, split lengthwise

9 egg yolks

¾ cup sugar

⅜ cup peanut butter, preferably smooth

FOR THE CRUSTS:

2 cups all-purpose flour

½ cup sugar

8 tablespoons (1 stick) cold unsalted butter,
cut into small pieces

2 egg yolks

1 tablespoon heavy cream

¼ teaspoon pure vanilla extract

FOR THE FILLING:

7 ounces bittersweet chocolate

2 tablespoons unsalted butter

7 eggs

½ cup sugar

¾ teaspoon pure vanilla extract

½ teaspoon salt

FOR THE SAUCE:

4 cups sugar

1½ cups red wine, Cabernet or another full-bodied wine

Makes about 24; can be halved

MAKE THE ICE CREAM: Heat the half-and-half and vanilla bean in a sauce-pan over medium heat, stirring occasionally to make sure the mixture doesn't scorch on the bottom. When the cream mixture reaches a fast sim-mer (do not let it boil), turn off the heat. Set the mixture aside to infuse for 10 to 15 minutes.

Whisk together the egg yolks and sugar in a medium bowl. Whisking constantly, slowly pour the hot half-and-half mixture into the egg yolk mix-ture. Return the mixture to the saucepan and cook over medium heat, stirring constantly with a wooden spoon. At 160 degrees, the mixture will give off a puff of steam. When the mixture reaches 180 degrees, it will be thickened and creamy, like eggnog. Test it by dipping a wooden spoon into the mixture. Run your finger down the back of the spoon. If the stripe remains clear, the mixture is ready; if the edges blur, the mixture is not quite thick enough yet. When it is ready, quickly remove it from the heat.

Immediately whisk in the peanut butter and whisk until smooth. Strain the mixture into a bowl to smooth it and remove the vanilla beam. Rest the bottom of the bowl in the ice bath and let the mixture cool, stirring often, for 2 hours. Freeze according to the directions of the ice-cream machine.

MAKE THE CRUSTS: In a mixer fitted with a paddle attachment (or using a hand mixer), mix the flour and sugar. Add the butter and mix until coarse and sandy.

Whisk the egg yolks, cream, and vanilla together. Add to the flour mix-ture and mix at low speed just until combined. If the mixture seems too dry, add another teaspoon of heavy cream. Turn the dough out onto a work surface and form into a disk. Wrap in plastic wrap and refrigerate for at least 1 hour, until ready to use. *(The recipe can be made up to this point and kept refrigerated for up to 2 days.)*

Roll out the dough ⅛ inch thick on a lightly floured surface and cut out circles that are 2 inches larger in diameter than the mini-muffin cups.

Spray the muffin tin well with nonstick cooking spray, then gently press the dough rounds into the cups, easing the dough completely into the cups. Smooth out the folds by pressing the dough against the sides and bottoms of the cups (the walls will become a little thicker). Use your fingers to form the rim of each tartlet into an even edge, pulling or cutting off extra bits of dough if necessary.

Spray the bottom of another mini-muffin tin with nonstick spray and gently push it down into the tin with the dough rounds so that it "spoons" into the bottom cups. This will help prevent shrinkage during baking. Chill for 30 minutes.

Heat the oven to 375 degrees. Keeping the tins pressed together, turn them upside down on a sheet pan. Bake until the crusts are dry and golden but not brown, about 12 minutes. Let them cool upside down for 20 minutes, then invert the pans and carefully lift the top tin out, leaving the pastry cups in the bottom tin.

Meanwhile, make the filling: Melt the chocolate and butter together in the top of a double boiler set over barely simmering water, stirring frequently. When melted, remove the mixture from the heat and whisk in the eggs, sugar, vanilla, and salt.

Heat the oven to 350 degrees. Pour the filling into the prebaked tart shells (still in their tins) and bake for 11 to 13 minutes, until the filling is set at the edges but still a little moist in the center.

Meanwhile, make the caramel sauce: Pour the sugar into the center of a deep saucepan. Carefully pour ½ cup water around the sugar, trying not to splash any sugar onto the sides of the pan. Do not stir; gently draw your finger through the center of the sugar to moisten it. Over high heat, bring the mixture to a full boil and cook without stirring, swirling the pot occasionally to even out the color, until it is amber-caramel, 10 to 20 minutes. When the mixture is done, immediately remove the pot from the heat. Use a wooden spoon to slowly stir in the red wine. Set aside.

When ready to serve, arrange the tarts on serving plates. Put a dollop of the sauce on the plate on one side of the tart and a small scoop of the ice cream on the other side. Serve immediately.

⤙ *R*OZANNE GOLD ⤚

BOOK: *Christmas 1-2-3*
EVENT MENU: Brie Croustades with Red Caviar,
Peppery Pecans, Sweet Garlic-Fennel Bisque, Sage-Roasted Capon
with Wild Mushrooms, Sugar Snaps in Orange Butter,
Red Cabbage with Honey and Vinegar, Olive Oil Mashed Potatoes,
Slow-Baked Pears with Stilton, Warm Honey Syrup

THE INTERNATIONAL ASSOCIATION OF CULINARY PROFESSIONALS (IACP) is an organization that holds a conference in a different North American city each year. I first met Rozanne Gold at the 2000 conference in Providence, Rhode Island. A year later, in March 2001, I heard that she was to be visiting Vancouver to tape a segment on a locally produced cooking show. I phoned Rozanne to see if we could host an event for her while she was in town. And as I was also planning to be in New York the following week, she suggested we have dinner together at Windows on the World. Normally I would never have gone to the World Trade Center, since I had at that time a tremendous fear of heights. But I wasn't about to pass up an evening with Chef Rozanne Gold and restaurant consultant Michael Whiteman, partners both in this fabled restaurant and in life, because of fear.

The evening was spectacular, and I was proud of myself for both facing and overcoming my fear. The prize was meeting two wonderful people. In May 2001, I was in New York again in the company of my sixteen-year-old niece. I calmly entered the World Trade Center and the two of us whirled skyward for lunch at Windows on the World compliments of Rozanne and Michael. After lunch I took my niece up the Empire State Building. Another first.

Rozanne has written a series of 1-2-3 books that feature recipes using no more than three ingredients. Sometimes, I think, people just don't believe you can achieve a memorable meal with so little, but Rozanne has proven that you can. When Rozanne and Michael came to Vancouver, we hosted an event to promote *Healthy 1-2-3*. The book, which contains an abundance of healthy information, is indeed a wonder.

Every year, at the shop, we have a few traditions. In December 2002, our annual Christmas event featured Rozanne's wee gem *Christmas 1-2-3*. What a great idea—simple yet festive recipes to see you through the hectic holiday season.

ROZANNE WRITES: Somewhere in a keepsake drawer lies a photograph of my husband and me. Our arms are wrapped around each other in an embrace so childlike and tender that one could only imagine us standing in an amusement park or at the departures lounge at Kennedy airport.

We were, in fact, in a bookstore, unexpectedly exuberant after a book signing that had been arranged for me. It was April, the wine was flowing (I'd never had wine from British Columbia before) and on a beautifully cool late afternoon, elegant couples, most of them as tall as me, came to say hello. Barbara-jo McIntosh, one of Canada's national treasures, was my host. Little did I know she was to become one of my closest friends.

Barbara-Jo's Books to Cooks has a kind of magic that is hard to escape. It is a candy store for grown-ups—with a dizzying selection of delicious titles that make you hunger. At Barbara-Jo's soirées, one's hunger is satisfied. The in-house chef made an impressive showing of the recipes from my cookbook. No one even suspected they were healthy! Most people focussed on the fact that all of the recipes used only three ingredients and they looked and tasted so good. I must admit I do love my food best when someone else makes it—especially when they make it much better than I do.

Why three ingredients, you ask? My search for a simpler path through the complexities of cuisine and nutrition has led me to eliminate the excesses of "gastronomy" that have proliferated in recent years. Limiting each recipe to three ingredients results in dishes that are freed from "flavour cover-up." It is my belief that simplicity can amplify the flavour of any dish—by letting the inherent qualities of the best ingredients speak for themselves.

BRIE CROUSTADES WITH RED CAVIAR

½ pound double-cream Brie cheese, chilled

3 extra-large eggs

½ cup salmon caviar

Makes 24

Cut rind from cheese using a small sharp knife. Discard rind. Let cheese sit at room temperature for 30 minutes. Meanwhile, preheat oven to 35 degrees.

Put eggs in bowl of a food processor. Cut cheese into 1-inch pieces and add to processor. Process until very smooth and thick, about 1 minute.

Coat two 12-hole, 2-inch diameter nonstick muffin pans with cooking spray. Spoon 1 tablespoon cheese mixture into each muffin cup. Bake for 9 to 10 minutes, until croustades are puffed and golden.

Let croustades sit for 1 minute, then remove from tins using a small flexible spatula. Top each slightly warm or room-temperature croustade with 1 teaspoon caviar. (Before topping with caviar, the croustades can be rewarmed: place in a pie pan, cover with foil, and heat for 3 minutes in a 325-degree oven. Serve within 20 minutes.)

PEPPERY PECANS

4 tablespoons unsalted butter

3 tablespoons Worcestershire sauce

4 cups shelled pecan halves, about 16 ounces

Makes about 4 cups

Preheat oven to 350 degrees. In a large nonstick skillet, melt butter and add 2 tablespoons Worcestershire sauce and lots of freshly ground black pepper. Add pecans and a large pinch of salt. Stir and cook over medium heat for 3 minutes, making sure the nuts are coated. Transfer to a baking sheet and bake for 12 minutes, stirring often. Drain on paper towels. Toss with more salt, pepper, and remaining Worcestershire sauce.

⤙ *J*OYCE GOLDSTEIN ⤚

BOOK: *Enoteca*
EVENT MENU: Frico, Code di scampi del Tirreno, Polpette al barese, Funghi trifolati, Panna cotta alla castagne

WHEN JOYCE GOLDSTEIN enters my kitchen, I get an immediate feeling of comfort. After all, Joyce has cooked for friends, family and the many patrons of her legendary San Francisco restaurant, Square One. So I know I'm going to witness a well-seasoned, intellectual woman work a special kind of culinary magic—a craft one can only hone after many years in the kitchen.

Joyce has been in the shop on three different occasions to promote her books. Although a new jewel seems to be published every year, *Enoteca* is one of my favourites. It never fails to bring back fond memories of a particular *enoteca* I visited in Siena. The recipes—like all of the food Joyce prepares—are authentic, interesting and delicious.

SHRIMP WRAPPED IN PANCETTA

(*Code di scampi del Tirreno*)
¾ cup extra-virgin olive oil
12 jumbo shrimp, peeled and deveined
¾ cup Cognac
12 paper-thin slices pancetta (not too lean)
Serves 4

Preheat oven to 475°F.

Warm the olive oil in a large sauté pan over medium-high heat. Add the shrimp and sauté quickly until they turn pink, about 3 minutes. Transfer to a plate. Add the Cognac and deglaze the pan, scraping up the brown bits on the pan bottom. Set the pan aside off the heat.

Wrap each shrimp in a slice of pancetta and arrange on a baking sheet. Place in the oven just long enough for the fat to start to melt, 2 to 3 minutes.

Meanwhile, reheat the pan juices. When the shrimp are ready, transfer them to 4 individual serving plates, top with the pan juices, and serve at once.

SAUTÉED MUSHROOMS
(Funghi trifolati)
Small handful (about ½ ounce) dried porcini mushrooms
5 tablespoons olive oil or equal parts unsalted butter and olive oil
1 tablespoon minced garlic
¼ cup diced pancetta or prosciutto (optional)
2 tablespoons chopped fresh nepitella or fresh mint, or equal parts chopped
fresh mint and oregano
1 pound mixed fresh mushrooms, sliced ¼ inch thick
½ cup dry white wine, if needed
¼ cup chopped fresh flat-leaf parsley
Salt and freshly ground black pepper
Serves 6 as an appetizer

Combine the dried porcini with hot water to cover in a bowl for 30 minutes. Drain, reserving the liquid. Chop the porcini finely and set aside. Pass the liquid through a cheesecloth-lined sieve and reserve.

Warm the olive oil or olive oil and butter in a large sauté pan over medium heat. Add the garlic and pancetta or prosciutto, if using, and sauté for 2 minutes. Raise the heat to high, add half of the *nepitella* or mint (or mint and oregano) and the mushrooms, and cook quickly until tender, 6 to 8 minutes. If the mushrooms have not given off much liquid, add the wine and cook quickly until the wine is absorbed. Add the chopped dried porcini along with the strained liquid and the remaining herbs. Stir well, sprinkle with salt and pepper, and heat through. Serve at once.

◄ *D*ONNA HAY ►

ON DONNA HAY'S second visit to the shop, her many fans were anxious to meet her. It all started with *The New Cook*. Then there were *Entertaining*, *New Food Fast* and *Flavours*. Why are Donna's books so popular? They're cleverly designed, beautifully photographed and deliciously affordable. Best of all, the recipes are fun and approachable.

I have stated more than once that the best way to entertain for Sunday lunch is to peruse one of Donna's books that morning, jot down the necessary ingredients and make a quick trip to the market before you can say "G'day." Lunch can be served by 1 PM. Donna's simple approach couldn't be more relaxing.

Donna has left her position as food editor of *Marie Claire* magazine to create a self-titled magazine of her own. Since that time, she's published her three latest books: *Off the Shelf*, *Modern Classics: Book One* and *Modern Classics: Book Two*. To date we have sold more than four thousand copies of the combined collection. Thank you, Donna, for paying the rent—more than once.

FRESH SALMON AND LIME CAKES
500 g (1 lb) salmon fillet, skin removed

1 egg white

3 tablespoons fine rice flour

2 kaffir lime leaves, shredded

1 tablespoon finely chopped ginger

1 tablespoon wasabi paste

3 tablespoons chopped fresh chervil or flat-leaf parsley

oil, to shallow-fry

LIME DIPPING SAUCE
¼ cup (2 fl oz) lime juice
¼ cup (2 fl oz) soy sauce
2 tablespoons brown sugar
Makes 20 small cakes

To make the salmon cakes, remove any bones from the salmon and chop into 5 mm (¼ inch) dice. Combine the chopped salmon with the egg white, rice flour, lime leaves, ginger, wasabi paste and chopped chervil or parsley.

Heat 1 cm (½ inch) of the oil in a frying pan over medium heat to shallow-fry the cakes. Place 2 tablespoons of the mixture into the hot oil and cook for 35–45 seconds each side, or until lightly golden. Drain on absorbent paper and keep warm in a low oven while you cook the rest.

To make the lime dipping sauce, combine the lime juice, soy sauce and sugar. Serve the dipping sauce with the warm salmon cakes and salad greens as a starter or main meal.

*K*EN HOM

BOOK: *Ken Hom: Travels With a Hot Wok*
EVENT MENU: Stir-fried Beef with Five Peppercorns

THROUGH ALL THE TRIALS and tribulations of creating a business, I never doubted my decision to open Barbara-Jo's Books to Cooks, but a wonderful seal of approval came very soon after the shop had become a reality. Stephen Wong, local food writer and Chinese culinary expert, was scouting locations for the BBC production *Ken Hom: Travels With a Hot Wok*. Due to inclement weather, an outside location for the Vancouver segment fell through. Luckily, I was at the shop late that evening when a frantic telephone call came from Stephen requesting a viewing of the shop for the director.

This visit led to a day of filming in the store with the most professional and wonderful group of "film types" one could ever hope to meet. Ken Hom was enthused by the selection of books (some of his many publications were on the shelf) and loved my kitchen. Kate Kinninmont—director extraordinaire—suggested that I be included in some of the frames and of course I was flattered. I allowed the makeup artist to powder my nose and then enthusiastically took my orders.

Months later, we started to see people from the U.K. wander through the shop stating they had seen me on British television. I accused the first person making this statement of lying, as I imagined my participation would have ended up on the cutting-room floor. But, alas, it was true. I can't say that a star was born, but the exposure made me feel as if I'd just found a gross of Perigord black truffles.

KEN WRITES: My BBC producer, Kate Kinninmont, had told me about a wonderful location that she found to film during our shoot in Vancouver. It was more than I expected: a relaxing, inviting shop called Barbara-Jo's Books to Cooks. The shelves were lined with all of my favourite cookery books and there was a serious kitchen to boot. This was the last leg of our trip and the shop was exactly what the crew and I needed. We all felt at home, beginning with Barbara-jo's welcoming smile. When the filming was finished, no one wanted to leave. We can't wait to return.

Ken prepared the following recipe that day. BBC productions being very particular, we ate a lot of this tasty dish over repeated takes.

STIR-FRIED BEEF WITH FIVE PEPPERCORNS

1 lb (450 g) lean beef steak

1 tablespoon light soy sauce

1 tablespoon Shaoxing rice wine or dry sherry

2 teaspoons cornstarch

2 teaspoons sesame oil

3 tablespoons oil, preferably peanut

2 tablespoons cognac

4 oz (100 g) shallots, finely chopped

2 tablespoons five-pepper mixture (see book for details), crushed

½ tsp salt

1 cup (250 ml) chicken stock

2 tablespoons (25 g) butter, cut in small pieces

Serves 4

Cut the beef into thick slices 2 × ¼ in (5 cm × 5 cm), cutting across the grain. Put the beef in a bowl with the soy sauce, rice wine or sherry, cornstarch and sesame oil. Mix well, and then let the mixture marinate for about 20 minutes.

Heat a wok or large frying-pan over a high heat. Add the oil, and when it is very hot and slightly smoking, remove the beef from the marinade with a slotted spoon. Add it to the pan and stir-fry it for about 2 minutes, until it is barely cooked. Remove and let it drain in a colander or sieve. Pour out all the oil, reheat the wok or a pan over a high heat, then add the cognac to deglaze. Quickly add the shallots, peppercorns, salt, and stock and reduce by half over a high heat. Finally, add the butter, piece by piece. Then return the beef to the wok or pan and stir-fry for 30 seconds to warm it through. Serve immediately.

≺ *N*ATHAN HYAM ≻

BOOK: *New Thai Cuisine*

EVENT MENU: Ginger and Mushroom Baked Coconut Rice,
Coconut Lemon Grass Baked Chicken,
Chili Garlic Beans with Cashews, Banana Mango Cake

NATHAN HYAM is a local chef who has spent a tremendous amount of time both travelling and living in Thailand. So I feel he is more than qualified to write a book about the cuisine of that country. As well, he has dedicated a good part of his career to educating the masses about the flavours of Thailand.

When Nathan launched his book at the shop, he came equipped with an impressive, custom-built propane wok. Both the wok and the event were a smashing success. But even without the grand wok, this book would be a welcome addition to your collection of Asian recipes.

COCONUT LEMON GRASS
BAKED CHICKEN

3 cloves garlic, minced

½ tsp. (2.5 mL) black peppercorns, crushed

¼ cup (60 mL) fish sauce

2 Tbsp. (30 mL) whiskey or brandy

1 Tbsp. (15 mL) Red Curry Paste (see recipe below)

3 Tbsp. (45 mL) finely chopped lemon grass

3 Tbsp. (45 mL) coconut milk

1 tsp. (5 mL) salt

3 lbs. (1.35 kg) chicken thighs

Serves 6

Combine all the ingredients except the chicken in a large bowl. Add the chicken and make sure it's well coated in the marinade. Marinate in the fridge for a minimum of 15 minutes and up to 10 hours.

Preheat the oven to 350°F (175°C).

Place the chicken on a baking sheet and bake for about 45 minutes, or until the meat is no longer pink when the thigh is sliced through to the bone.

Serve with Sweet Chili Sauce (recipe follows).

RED CURRY PASTE

15 dried hot chili peppers

1 two-inch (5-cm) cube fresh galanga root

2 stalks lemon grass

2 Tbsp. (30 mL) coriander seeds

2 Tbsp. (30 mL) cumin seeds

4 tsp. (20 mL) paprika

¼ tsp. (1.2 mL) turmeric

¼ tsp. (1.2 mL) cinnamon

3½ inch (1.2 cm) pieces lime rind, finely chopped

6 shallots (or ½ onion), chopped

5 cilantro roots, cleaned and diced (or 10 stems)

6 cloves garlic, chopped

1½ tsp. (7.5 mL) shrimp paste

½ red bell pepper, diced

Remove and discard the seed from the chili peppers (if you want a milder paste). Cover with warm water and soak for 30 minutes.

Peel and chop the galanga. Finely slice the lemon grass, discarding the top and root.

Roast the coriander and cumin together in a frying pan over medium heat until a little smoke rises from the seeds (a few minutes). Grind in a mortar and pestle then add the paprika, turmeric and cinnamon.

Drain the chilies, saving the liquid. Purée the chilies with all the other ingredients in a blender or processor until a fine paste is achieved. The texture should be similar to soft peanut butter. Use the chili water to thin the paste if necessary.

SWEET CHILI SAUCE

4 tsp. (20 mL) oil

1 medium onion, diced

8 cloves garlic, diced

2 fresh red chilies, diced, or dried chilies, soaked and diced

1 red bell pepper, diced

⅓ cup (80 mL) palm or brown sugar

2 Tbsp. (30 mL) fish sauce

2 Tbsp. (30 mL) rice vinegar

1 cup (240 mL) water

1 cup (240 mL) chicken or vegetable stock

Makes 2½ cups (600 mL)

Heat 2 tsp. (10 mL) of the oil in a saucepan over medium heat, and sauté the onion, garlic, chilies and red pepper until lightly browned.

Place ⅔ of the sautéed mixture in a blender, add the sugar, fish sauce and vinegar and purée until smooth.

Heat the remaining 2 tsp. (10 mL) of oil over high heat. Return the puréed mixture to the pan with the remaining sautéed vegetables and sauté the mixture for a couple of minutes. Add the water and stock, then bring to a boil. Cool before using.

Note: The taste can be varied by adding more water, or extra sugar or chilies. To make a thicker sauce, mix together 1 Tbsp. (15 mL) cornstarch and 3 Tbsp. (45 mL) cold water. Stir it into the sauce and bring to a boil.

⤙ RAGHAVAN IYER ⤚

BOOK: *The Turmeric Trail*

EVENT MENU: Potato Croquettes with Lime Juice,
Unripe Papaya Salad with Chilies, Shrimp with Cream and Fennel,
Basmati Rice with Saffron and Rose Petals, Assorted Bell Peppers with
Roasted Garbanzo Bean Flour, Sweetened Yogurt with Mangoes

HAVE YOU EVER WITNESSED the proper way to grate a coconut? Well, when Raghavan Iyer leapt to the counter of my kitchen in a single bound and positioned himself on a bench-like stool with a grater attached to the end of it, I most certainly did. I must confess that my heart skipped a few beats in the process.

Charm oozes from this elegant Indian and, in his presence, you are taken to another place. That evening in the shop, he read from his cookbook, *The Turmeric Trail*—sharing with us stories that have shaped his life—and prepared food that has nurtured his soul. As the night ended, we were wrapped in a romantic web—spun by a man who lives to share his passion.

Jan Dicks is a woman who has attended over one hundred events at the shop and she has remarked on more than one occasion that this was her most memorable visit. Truly, it was an evening to cherish.

UNRIPE PAPAYA SALAD WITH CHILIES
(*Kaccu Papaya Nu Salade*)

Choose a papaya that is green, firm, and unripe. Peel it with a potato peeler or a paring knife. The flesh will be light green in color (unlike the orange red color when ripe). Slice the papaya lengthwise, and with a spoon scoop out and discard the pearl-like white seeds (which will turn a beautiful black color when ripe). Use the slicer blade attachment of a food processor to slice the papaya thin; a box grater's slicer surface will also suffice.

1 medium green (unripe) papaya, peeled,
seeded, and thinly sliced (see note)
Juice of 1 large lime
2 tablespoons finely chopped fresh cilantro
1 teaspoon salt
1 teaspoon sugar
¼ teaspoon ground turmeric
3 to 4 fresh Thai, cayenne, or serrano chilies, slit open lengthwise
1 tablespoon vegetable oil
1 teaspoon black mustard seed
¼ teaspoon hing (asafetida)
Serves 4

1. In a medium bowl, combine the papaya, lime juice, cilantro, salt, sugar, turmeric, and chilies. Mix well.
2. In a small skillet, heat the oil over medium-high heat; add the mustard seed. When it begins to pop, cover the skillet. As soon as the seed finishes popping, add the hing and sizzle for 2 to 5 seconds. Pour the seed-oil mixture over the papaya and toss well to coat. Serve chilled or at room temperature.

⤙ $\mathcal{B}$ ILL JONES ⤞

BOOK: *Sublime Vegetarian*

EVENT MENU: Assorted Vegetarian Sushi, Chilled Carrot, Kaffir Lime and Ginger Custard with Green Curry Sauce, Goat's Cheese, Corn and Shiitake Mushroom Quiche with Savoury Rice Crust, Pear and Lychee Tarte Tatin

BILL JONES IS A most imposing figure. When meeting him in civvies, you would not immediately spot him as a chef. You might agree that his first career choice of geologist seems more appropriate. Lucky for us, he chose arranging ingredients over sorting rocks.

Although I'm a big fan of his recipes, I most enjoy him when he's educating us about various ingredients. I have been fortunate enough to go mushroom foraging with Bill. He can spot a wee morsel yards away, bound eagerly to it and tell you everything you need to know about it.

When Bill comes to teach at the shop, he arrives with bags full of wonderful stuff. I always get excited as I watch him place his treasure on the counter because I know I am going to be introduced to great ideas I can take home to my kitchen.

Bill has six cookbooks to his credit and although he isn't a vegetarian, *Sublime Vegetarian* is my personal favourite. When the book was published we had a media launch at the shop. With meals this tasty, it is easy to forget about meat.

CHILLED CARROT, KAFFIR LIME AND GINGER CUSTARD WITH GREEN CURRY SAUCE

CARROT, KAFFIR LIME AND GINGER CUSTARD:

2 cups (500 mL) vegetable stock or water

2 cups (500 mL) carrots, sliced

1 kaffir lime leaf (or zest of 1 lime)

1 Tb (15 mL) ginger, minced

2 whole eggs (or 3 egg whites)

½ cup (125 mL) yogurt (or sour cream)

salt and pepper to taste

GREEN CURRY SAUCE:

1 Tb (15 mL) vegetable oil

1 Tb (15 mL) garlic, minced

1 cup (250 mL) onions, diced

2 tsp (10 mL) curry paste

1 cup (250 mL) vegetable stock or water

1 cup (250 mL) spinach leaves

salt and pepper to taste

small spinach leaves for garnish

Serves 4

TO MAKE CUSTARD

Preheat oven to 325°F (160°C).

1. In a saucepan, combine stock, carrots, kaffir lime leaf and ginger. Bring to a boil, then reduce the heat and simmer for 15 minutes, or until the carrots are soft. Remove from the heat and allow to cool.

2. Use a slotted spoon to transfer carrots to a blender or food processor, reserving liquid. Discard kaffir lime leaf. While blending, add liquid slowly until smooth. Transfer to a small bowl, then whisk in eggs and yogurt. Season well with salt and pepper.

3. Spoon the carrot mixture into 4 lightly oiled individual custard dishes and place in a shallow roasting pan. Fill the pan with boiling water to ½ the height of the custard dishes. Cover the pan with foil and bake in the oven for 30 minutes, or until custard is just set. Remove from the oven and place on a cooling rack. Remove the custard dishes from the water when possible and let cool to room temperature. Chill in the refrigerator for at least 30 minutes before serving.

TO MAKE SAUCE

4. In a saucepan, heat vegetable oil. Add garlic and onions. Sauté over medium-high heat for 3 to 4 minutes, or until soft and beginning to brown. Add curry paste, stirring well to coat, and cook for 2 to 3 minutes, or until fragrant. Pour

in stock and bring to a boil. Toss in the spinach, stirring, for about 1 minute, or until it wilts and turns deep green. Transfer to a blender or food processor and purée. Add more liquid if necessary to form a light sauce. Season with salt and pepper. Set aside.

5. To serve, run a sharp knife around the rim of one custard dish. With a quick motion, flip the custard dish upside-down over a plate, allowing the custard to slide out (tap gently to coax it out). Repeat with the remaining custards. Pour the curry sauce around each custard and garnish with spinach leaves.

ℰMERIL LAGASSE

BOOK: *Emeril's TV Dinners*
EVENT MENU: Sweet Potato and Pecan Pie

I HAVE BEEN FORTUNATE to receive a tremendous amount of support from publishers when it comes to arranging for popular authors to come visit. Of course, it's frustrating when a publisher decides to give a chain bookstore the exclusive rights to a travelling author. Such was the case with Emeril Lagasse. But, as luck would have it, he made an appearance at the shop anyway. To this day, I'm not sure who orchestrated a TV interview with Emeril and Jill Krop in my shop, but I will always be grateful.

Emeril's visit was short but wonderfully sweet. He was generous with his compliments about the shop, commenting that we had a renowned reputation. Best of all, he took time out from his hectic schedule to speak with a crowd of fans who had gathered outside the window while the cameras were rolling. We rewarded him with a piece of Sweet Potato and Pecan Pie, his recipe from *Emeril's TV Dinners*. He was delighted.

SWEET POTATO AND PECAN PIE

1 pound sweet potatoes, scrubbed

1 tablespoon olive oil

Salt and freshly ground black pepper to taste

½ cups Steen's 100% Pure Cane Syrup

1 teaspoon ground cinnamon

½ teaspoon ground ginger

½ teaspoon freshly grated nutmeg

5 large eggs

1½ teaspoons pure vanilla extract

1 unbaked 10-inch Basic Savory Piecrust
(see book for details)

1½ cups pecan pieces

½ cup granulated sugar

½ cup firmly packed light brown sugar

¼ cup light corn syrup

Pinch of salt
½ cup Chocolate Sauce (see book for details), warmed slightly
1 cup Sweetened Whipped Cream (see book for details)
Confectioners' sugar
Makes one 10-inch pie; 8 servings

Preheat the oven to 375°F. Place the sweet potatoes on a baking sheet and drizzle with the olive oil. Season with salt and pepper. Bake until they are fork tender, 1 to 1½ hours. Cool, peel, and mash.

In a large mixing bowl, combine the potatoes, the Steen's syrup, the spices, 1 of the eggs, and ½ teaspoon of the vanilla. Mix well. Line a 10-inch deep-dish pie pan with the rolled-out pie dough, then pour the filling into the pastry shell. Spread the pecan pieces evenly over the filling.

In another large mixing bowl, combine the remaining 4 eggs, remaining 1 teaspoon vanilla, granulated sugar, brown sugar, corn syrup, and salt and stir to blend. Pour over the pecans. Bake until the filling sets and the pastry is nicely browned, about 1 hour.

Remove from the oven and cool for 10 minutes before slicing to serve. Garnish with chocolate sauce, whipped cream, and confectioners' sugar.

⊰ 𝒻RIEND OF THE SHOP: ⊱
JOHN LEKICH
*John Lekich is an author and film critic who once indulged
in a cocktail with George Plimpton before noon.*

JOHN LEKICH WRITES: In the heart of every great bookstore, there's an oasis that feels as if it's been created just for you. It's some little nook or cranny where you can connect with a subject so tantalizing that it provides passage to a whole other world. There's a place like that for me at Barbara-Jo's Books to

Cooks. I call it cocktail corner because it features books that reveal the sleek mysteries behind such exotic libations as Between the Sheets and Satan's Whiskers. One part commerce and two parts magic, cocktail corner is close enough to the cash register to hear the discreet ring of customers purchasing serious works on an endless variety of culinary subjects. But all it takes is a few seconds of mulling over the heady recipe for something like The Mule's Hind Leg before that very sound begins to resemble the happy clink of ice against glass.

My fascination with cocktails began at a precocious age. I blame an early exposure to *The Thin Man* movies. A sublime concoction that began in the 1930s and unfurled like a dazzling string of pearls into the next decade, the series featured William Powell and Myrna Loy as detectives Nick and Nora Charles. Nick and Nora lived in a world of book-lined dens, overnight train trips and perfectly chilled martinis. Although every movie did feature at least one unfortunate murder, the brandishing of highballs outnumbered gunshots by a ratio of at least ten to one. The opening scene of *The Thin Man* shows Nick offering reverent instruction on how to create the ideal martini. "Always have rhythm in your shaking," he advises. "A dry martini you always shake to waltz time." Even as a kid, I knew it was great advice. Just as I knew that I'd somehow missed an invitation to the great cocktail waltz by more than a few decades.

It was Barbara-jo who taught me that the waltz isn't over. You just have to learn to listen for the music in different places. I discovered this by walking through the door of Barbara-Jo's Books to Cooks the very first time. If you have a dream that involves sipping or tasting in an elegant setting, it's approachable in any number of ways. One of my favourites involves perusing such nostalgic volumes as *Esquire's Handbook for Hosts* and *The Gentleman's Companion Volume II*, two books I discovered in the store's vintage section, which flows into cocktail corner like gin kissing vermouth.

I now have a collection of cocktail books that goes a long way toward satisfying my thirst for glamour. I keep the volumes piled by my bedside. And sometimes, when I can't sleep, I'll mull over pictures of frosted glasses and cocktail shakers in the shape of penguins. Once in a while I'll whisper the name of an especially exotic ingredient or laugh at a vintage *New Yorker* cartoon that takes place between some sad-eyed commuter and a knowing bartender. In the still of the night, it's remarkably comforting.

But nothing can top the adventure of actually drinking a cocktail in cocktail corner. A totally unique experience—made possible by the shop's fully working kitchen—this blissful marriage of theory and practice took place during a class on the history and preparation of the venerable martini. Surrounded by cherished books—chilled glass in hand—I felt just like Nick Charles. Someone inquired about my thoughts on the martini, and I was ready. "Always shake it gently," I smiled. "To the tempo of a waltz."

⤞ Sarah McLachlan ⤝
(Jaime Laurita, Contributor)
BOOK: *Plenty*
EVENT MENU: Spicy Spring Rolls, Samosas,
Vegetable Sushi, Love Cake

VANCOUVER'S OWN Sarah McLachlan lives a life that most of us can only dream about. As well as being a sensation on the pop charts, Sarah truly believes in eating sensibly. When she travels around the globe, she wisely takes along a talented chef to keep her well nourished.

Chef Jaime Laurita has travelled with Sarah since 1997. They decided to write a book together to share their most memorable meals with us. Sarah is predominantly a vegetarian but enjoys eating fish on occasion, so I like to refer to *Plenty* as a pescetarian cookbook.

When I was asked to host a book signing for the release of *Plenty* I was ecstatic. As expected, the crowds thronged to meet Sarah and completely took over my little shop. We had to find room in my neighbour's space for the television and print media to have a quiet moment with our shining star. It was one of the shop's more hectic events. But I'd do it again in a second.

LOVE CAKE

1 cup vegetable shortening

1½ cups sugar

2 eggs

2 tablespoons cocoa powder

¼ cup beet juice

a few drops red food colouring

(optional)

½ teaspoon salt

1 teaspoon vanilla

1 cup buttermilk

2¼ cups flour (sifted three times)

1 tablespoon vinegar

1 teaspoon baking soda

Serves 10

Preheat oven to 350°F.

Grease two 9 inch round cake tins.

Cream shortening and sugar together until light and fluffy. Add eggs and beat 1 minute. In a separate bowl, mix cocoa powder, beet juice, food colouring and salt together to form a paste. Add to the shortening mixture and stir until well blended. Mix vanilla and buttermilk together and add alternately to the shortening mixture with the flour, about a third at a time.

Mix vinegar and baking soda together in a cup and add to the batter. Gently stir just until blended. Bake for 30 minutes. Cool cake in pans for 10 minutes; remove from pans and continue cooling on racks.

ICING

1 cup milk

7 tablespoons flour

1 cup butter, softened

1 cup icing sugar, sifted

1 teaspoon vanilla

Mix milk and flour together and cook over medium heat until thick. Refrigerate until completely cool.

Beat butter until light and fluffy. Gradually add sugar. Stir in vanilla. Add cooled milk mixture a little at a time and blend.

⤙ *F*RIENDS OF THE SHOP: ⤚
JAMIE MAW, MURRAY McMILLAN,
GLENYS MORGAN
FEATURED BOOK: *The New Food Lover's Companion*

EVERY SO OFTEN I like to use creative licence and throw a unique event to promote a book that I admire. When Sharon Tyler Herbst published a third edition of the highly popular *Food Lover's Companion*, I decided my only option was to host an evening of *Jeopardy!*—and position myself as the Alex Trebek of food trivia—with a wee gaggle of well-known food personalities.

I asked Jamie Maw, food and travel writer, to write a few words about his recollections of the evening and, as you see, he has not left much for me to say:

"How about asking more boy questions," I shouted politely at Barbara-jo McIntosh. I was turning crimson, by degrees Fahrenheit, then Celsius. Barbara-Jo's is not a place that I associate with the Inquisition. But that's precisely what I was getting that night, in gallons, cups and pecks—and then their metric equivalents. And the only humour that I could mobilize to rescue my deepening humiliation was, necessarily, of the deeply self-deprecating kind.

Several months before, I had signed on to participate in a sort of culinary Olympiad. The format: Answer—and answer quickly—any and all questions based on our study of the Barron's *Food Lover's Companion*, a seven-hundred-page brick thick with food, wine and culinary definitions. In fact any definition, from the more than four thousand in the book, was up for grabs. And my competitors were hardly flyweights: Murray McMillan, the well-travelled (and well-fed) food editor of *The Vancouver Sun*, and Glenys Morgan. Glenys owned a leading cookshop, cooked professionally for many years and then, most famously, trained hundreds of chefly aspirants at the Dubrulle School of the Culinary Arts and Deep Tissue Massage. Even worse, all of this was in front of a paying crowd, many eager to see one or more of us self-flambé. As a serial procrastinator, during the trip to Acapulco (on assignment, of course) that immediately preceded the competition, I had put any reflection on the now loathsome Barron's off completely. Or almost. Like reading *War and Peace*, I was still stuck in the first chapter, or in this case, the "A's"—trying to assimilate asafoetida [ah-sah-FEH-teh-dah], "a flavoring obtained from a giant fennellike plant that grows mainly in Iran and India . . .," and atemoya [a-teh-MOH-ee-yah], "though it's cultivated in Florida, this cross between CHERIMOYA and SWEETSOP is a native of South America and the West Indies. About the size of a large sweet BELL PEPPER, the atemoya has a tough dusty green skin . . ."

In short, my modest brain, now addled into prune whip by Mexican heat and humidity, was not up to the job. I very nearly sent Barbara-jo an urgent missive, but no—I swore to myself—I'd get cracking on the flight home. And I did, making it clear into the "B's" before breaking for a snooze somewhere over Manzanillo.

"Question one," began our Inquisitor, Barbara-jo McIntosh, herself no slouch at this sort of thing, but tonight looking much more headmistress than bookshop proprietor. "What is asafoetida?" I rang my bell instantly, barely beating out Glenys. "Though it's cultivated in Florida, this cross between…" I began. "Wrong," said Headmistress McIntosh. "Glenys, would you like to correct our tanned friend?"

And so it went. Murray and I split pretty evenly on male-friendly words like banger, hardtack, poutine, groundnut and yabbie. But Glenys grabbed everything else: corn salad, conchiglie, dragée, tzimmes, verjus and zuccotto. And many more. By the end of round one, Glenys had easily doubled Murray's and my collective score.

Then it got much worse: we broke into a lengthy series of baking questions. Baking questions! My baking repertoire is limited to Irish soda bread.

For my annual apple pie I follow the pastry recipe on the back of the shortening box. And that's when I measure at all. "What is an acceptable substitution for one cup of sifted, self-rising flour?" the headmistress barked. "One cup sifted all-purpose flour plus 1½ teaspoons baking powder and ⅛ teaspoon salt," Glenys promptly answered. "What is the volume of an 8″× 8″× 2″ square pan?" Eight cups, as it turns out. Of course, Glenys knew that too. That's when I rudely demanded that Headmistress McIntosh ask some more boy questions. But it was not to be. Instead, definitions and preparatory techniques for burdock, granadilla, kibbeh, ugli fruit (Murray and I worked that one to death, but were both wrong), varak (we had clearly moved beyond the B's now), and wakame and lassi ("A leading brand of American dog food?" I volunteered), followed faster than the 101st Airborne going downtown.

Needless to say, Murray and I were largely blanked, only responding to male-sensitive questions such as infusion, offal and roux. "Proper noun or not?" I enquired about roux, hoping for a bonus point for naming the founders of Le Gavroche and The Waterside Inn. "Not," replied the headmistress. One point only for the application of heat to butter and flour—a gimme. But by now, it was more rue than roux for Murray and me. Just to make sure, the headmistress consulted the chief scorekeeper (Adrienne O'Callaghan, who measures when she bakes) at unnecessarily short intervals. By now, Glenys's score threatened to triple our aggregate.

One final chance for redemption. "What is Spam, and, part two—where in the world is it most consumed?" the headmistress demanded. I rang my bell furiously. Finally. I know quite a lot about pork products and even have a Spam snow dome on my desk. "Spam is a prepared pork product manufactured by the Hormel Corporation that chiefly informs the diet of the state of Hawaii," I fairly screamed. "It is occasionally used in sculpture competitions," I added. Two points, too late. The event was over, the humiliation final and brutish. I could barely choke down my thoroughly chilled beverage. To this day I feel little affection for asafoetida.

I congratulated Glenys thoroughly on the new automobile she won, and she congratulated us for being such good sports. Our prizes were brand new copies of the Barron's *Food Lover's Companion*. I'll use mine to keep the back door open on breezy days. When I'm cooling down my annual apple pie. After escaping the amazingly sympathetic crowd, I asked Headmistress McIntosh how the questions could have been so transparently one-sided—so, well, *girly*. "Couldn't you have balanced things by asking for stuff like spice rub, condiments of leading steakhouses of the U.S. Midwest, pickled herring, vindaloo and the best places to eat barbecue in Kansas City?" I asked. "And you know I don't measure," I said. "It's never too late to start," the headmistress said firmly, and with the absolute conviction of those who do.

⤜ *F*RANÇOIS PAYARD ⤛

BOOK: *Simply Sensational Desserts*
EVENT MENU: Poached Pears in Caramel Passion Sauce with
Honey Ice Cream and Arlette, Lemon Tart, Chocolate Pudding Cake,
Pistachio-Almond Biscotti, Warm Chocolate Tart

ONE DAY, it occurred to me that it would be really great to have François Payard come to visit. He had just published *Simply Sensational Desserts*. It is the perfect book for the many customers who visit the shop just to purchase books from our sweets section. So I stated (rather presumptuously) that I would telephone François and ask him to come. Jessica and Adrienne were taken aback by my brashness, but it turned out to be one of the best decisions I ever made. Our initial conversation went something like this:

BJ: Hello, may I speak with François Payard.
FP: Allo.
BJ: Is this François Payard?
FP: Oui.
BJ: Well, my name is Barbara-jo and I have a cookbook shop in Vancouver, Canada. I would love for you to visit us and promote your book.

FP: When?

BJ: In the autumn.

FP: No, the winter is better.

BJ: I will be in New York in September and I will come to meet you.

FP: Good.

When I went to visit François at his tony Manhattan patisserie, I was treated royally. I was shown a seat and asked to wait—but not without a glass of champagne, a wee bit of foie gras, caviar and a trio of pastries. A date was set for February and I floated back to my hotel.

When the time came for François to visit, the shop was packed with an excited group of guests. François, the consummate showman, was ready to deliver. We had a lot of fun. Jessica, a determined nine-to-fiver, was overwhelmed when François demanded she stay that evening to attend his class. We all had a good chuckle when she appeared, coyly, for the event.

I visit Payard Manhattan (for lunch or tea) every time I go to New York. François, who relishes his title of Pastry King (while clearly deserving a broader culinary reputation), greets me with the same words on every occasion. "When are you coming for dinner?"

WARM CHOCOLATE TART

8 ounces (227 grams) bittersweet chocolate, finely chopped

¾ cup (174 grams) heavy cream

½ cup (121 grams) whole milk

1 large egg, lightly beaten

One 9½-inch tart shell made from

Sweet Tart Dough (recipe below), prebaked

Makes 6 to 8 servings

1. Preheat the oven to 325°F.
2. Place the chopped chocolate in a medium bowl and set aside.
3. Combine the cream and milk in a medium saucepan, and bring to a boil over medium-high heat. Pour the hot cream mixture over the chocolate. Allow to stand for 30 seconds to melt the chocolate, then whisk until the chocolate is completely melted and the mixture is smooth. Allow to cool for 10 minutes.
4. Whisk the egg into the chocolate mixture. Pour the filling into the prebaked tart shell.
5. Bake the tart for 8 to 10 minutes, until the edges of the filling are set; the center will still be soft. Cool the tart on a wire rack for 10 minutes and serve warm.

SWEET TART DOUGH

1 cup plus 1 tablespoon (122 grams) confectioners' sugar
1¾ cups (254 grams) all-purpose flour
Pinch of salt
9 tablespoons (127 grams) unsalted butter, softened
1 large egg
Makes two 9½-inch tart shells

1. Sift together the confectioners' sugar, flour, and salt into a bowl.

2. Place the butter in a food processor and process until smooth, about 15 seconds. Scatter the flour mixture over the butter, add the egg, and process just until the dough forms a mass; do not overmix. Turn the dough out onto the counter and divide it in two. Shape each half into a disc, wrap in plastic wrap, and refrigerate for at least 2 hours or up to 24 hours. Half of the dough may be well wrapped and frozen for up to 1 month.

3. Let the dough stand at room temperature for 30 minutes to soften. Lightly butter two 9½-inch fluted tart pans with removable bottoms.

4. Dust a work surface lightly with flour. Dust one of the discs lightly with flour and, using a floured rolling pin, roll it out into a rough 12-inch circle. Lift the dough often, making sure that the work surface and dough are lightly floured at all times. Roll the dough up onto the rolling pin and gently unroll it over one of the prepared tart pans. Press the dough into the pan and roll the pin over the top of the pan to remove the excess dough. Repeat with the remaining dough and tart pan. Prick the bottom of the tart shells all over with a fork. Chill the tart shells for 20 minutes. (The tart shells can be refrigerated for up to 24 hours.)

TO PARTIALLY BAKE THE TART SHELLS: Pr3eheat the oven to 325°F. Lightly butter two pieces of aluminum foil large enough to generously line each tart pan. Line the tart shells with the foil, buttered side down, and fill with dried beans, rice, or pie weights.

Bake the tart shells for 15 minutes. Remove the foil and beans and continue baking for 5 minutes, until just set; the tart shells should have little or no color. Cool completely on a wire rack.

TO PREBAKE THE TART SHELLS: Preheat the oven to 325°F. Lightly butter two pieces of aluminium foil large enough to generously line each tart pan. Line the tart shells with the foil, buttered side down, and fill with dried beans, rice, or pie weights.

Bake the tart shells for 15 minutes. Remove the foil and beans and continue baking for 8 to 10 minutes longer, until evenly golden brown. Cool completely on a wire rack.

⤙ JAMES PETERSON ⤚

BOOK: *Splendid Soups*

EVENT MENU: Medieval Pea Soup with Ginger, Saffron and Almonds, Indian-Style Shrimp and Coconut Soup, Moroccan-Style Lamb Soup with Dried Apricots, Chicken Soup with Apples and Leeks

THE MANY CULINARY ADVENTURES of James Peterson have led to a singular career as a master cookbook writer. Along the way he has been there (owned a restaurant, lived and worked in the kitchens of France, spent quality time with the likes of Richard Olney) and done that (garnering a firm grasp of taste, technique and trends). Most of his books—*Splendid Soups, Sauces, Vegetables, Glorious French Food*—are mighty tomes of information. But others—*Simply Salmon* and *The Duck Cookbook,* for example—cover his chosen subject in a small but complete package.

James has come to visit us on two occasions, the first when *Splendid Soups* was revised. Once a year, I like to host an event at the shop for a worthy cause. It made perfect sense to combine an introduction to James Peterson and his book *Splendid Soups* with a charity event for A Loving Spoonful, an organization that delivers hot meals to at-home AIDS patients. The shop became an elegant soup kitchen and four wonderful chefs served four splendid soups. James demonstrated the Indian-Style Shrimp and Coconut Soup, but my favourite recipe that evening was the Moroccan-Style Lamb Soup with Dried Apricots prepared by David Hawksworth.

MOROCCAN-STYLE LAMB SOUP
WITH DRIED APRICOTS

4 lamb shanks, cut in half crosswise by the butcher,
trimmed of fat, or 1¼ pounds lamb shoulder,
cut into ¾-inch cubes

¼ cup olive oil

4 garlic cloves

2½ quarts chicken, beef, or lamb broth or water

1 medium-size onion, finely chopped

2 garlic cloves, finely chopped

1 teaspoon ground turmeric or 2 teaspoons
finely chopped fresh

A ¼-inch slice of fresh ginger, peeled and
finely chopped, or ½ teaspoon ground

Pinch of saffron

1 4-inch cinnamon stick or 1 teaspoon ground

6 medium-size tomatoes, peeled, seeded,
and chopped or 3 cups canned, seeded and drained

1 cup dried apricots

30 pearl onions, peeled

½ cup slivered almonds

1 tablespoon finely chopped cilantro leaves

1 tablespoon finely chopped fresh mint leaves

salt

pepper

¼ cup white wine vinegar

Makes 12 first-course or 6 main-course servings

In a 4-quart pot over high heat, brown the lamb in half the olive oil. Turn down the heat and drain off the burned fat. Add the unpeeled garlic cloves and broth. Bring to a slow simmer, cover, and simmer the lamb for 2½ to 3 hours. Use a ladle to skim off any fat or froth that floats to the top. If there isn't enough liquid to cover the shanks, turn them around in the liquid halfway into the cooking. You may also need to add more broth or water from time to time to make up for evaporation.

In a 4-quart pot over medium heat, cook the onion and finely chopped garlic in the remaining olive oil for about 5 minutes. Add the turmeric, ginger, and saffron and cook the mixture for 5 minutes more.

Add the cinnamon, tomatoes, dried apricots, and pearl onions to the spice mixture and strain in the liquid from the lamb shanks. Simmer gently for about 20 minutes.

Remove the meat from the lamb shanks, discarding any pieces of fat, bone, or cartilage. Cut the meat into small cubes and add it to the soup.

Preheat the oven to 375°F and lightly toast the slivered almonds for about 15 minutes.

A minute before serving, remove and discard the cinnamon stick, stir the chopped cilantro and mint along with the vinegar into the soup, and season with salt and pepper. Ladle the soup into wide bowls and sprinkle the toasted almonds over it.

⤚ *G*ORDON RAMSAY ⤛

BOOK: *A Chef for All Seasons*
EVENT MENU: Salt Cod Pâté with Cherry Tomato Dressing,
Tomato and Parmesan Gratinée Tarts, Saffron Scented Leek Soup with
Pickled Girolles, Pear, Honey and Lime Cake

WHEN WHITECAP BOOKS telephoned unexpectedly to say that the famous—and famously macho—Gordon Ramsay would be touring Canada, I was initially delighted. But after some reflection (followed by a strong drink), I realized that orchestrating an event could prove far more challenging than usual. We generally organize events three to five months in advance, since there are numerous decisions to be made, especially when working with culinary royalty. But everything went surprisingly well. A menu was chosen and Gordon conceded fairly easily to Adrienne (a female chef!) cooking his food. Needless to say, the event sold out instantly.

On the morning of his appearance, the telephone rang. It was Gordon, calling from New York. He had missed his flight and was not sure what to do. He blamed the setback on New York's most famous restaurateur, Daniel Boulud—as if that would ease the pain and make it okay for him to cancel. I calmly told him to get on the next available flight and explained that I would

meet him at the airport. He protested that the plane would get in too late. But I countered that I would postpone the event until his arrival. We both agreed that this was the best solution. So I telephoned thirty-five guests and asked them to come later. They were all kind enough to accommodate me.

Gordon arrived (without luggage, or having had a bath or a shave). His patient fans got just what they anticipated—a masterful cook who offered colourful opinions on media, women and his distaste for lily-livered, weak-kneed individuals. To my pleasant surprise, he was most complimentary about the way Adrienne (still female) had prepared his recipes for the event. The only critique—not enough salt. And with that, he was off to the pub for a few pints with the lads.

SALT COD PÂTÉ WITH
CHERRY TOMATO DRESSING

300g fillet of cod

60g sea salt flakes

A few fresh parsley stocks, twisted

2 good pinches of curry powder

1 tablespoon olive oil

1 medium waxy potato (such as Maris Piper),
peeled and diced

300ml milk

1 fat clove garlic, crushed

1 tablespoon chopped fresh parsley

100ml double cream

sea salt and freshly ground black pepper

DRESSING:

200g naturally ripened cherry tomatoes

½ teaspoon caster sugar

100ml groundnut or olive oil, plus extra for drizzling

1 tablespoon Dijon mustard

Serves 4 as a starter

1. Lay the cod in a shallow dish and sprinkle over the salt and parsley stalks. Cover the fish with cling film, then press a heavy plate on top. Chill for 24 hours, turning once, by which time you will find liquid oozing out and the fish firmed up.

2. Drain, rinse in cold water and pat dry. Discard the parsley stalks. The cod fillet should now weigh about 200g.

3. Cut the cod into large chunks and dust with curry powder. Heat the oil in a non-stick frying pan and sauté the cod until a good golden brown and quite firm. It is best overcooked slightly. Drain, cool and flake. Set aside.

4. Cook the potato in the milk with the crushed garlic and seasoning. Drain well, reserving some of the milk. Blend to a purée in a food processor (one of the few times when I do allow this!). If the mixture is a bit thick, trickle in some of the saved milk.

5. Cool the potato, then mix in the flaked cod and parsley. Whip the cream until it holds soft peaks. Fold into the cod mixture. Check the seasoning. Chill the mixture in a bowl should you wish to shape it into quenelles, or just press into ramekins and mark the top with the tip of a knife or tines of a fork.

6. For the dressing, whiz the tomatoes to a purée in a food processor. Press the purée through a sieve into a bowl, rubbing with the back of a ladle. Mix in the sugar, oil, mustard and seasoning. That's it. There is no need for any vinegar as the tomatoes are acid enough. (This makes 200ml, which leaves plenty of extra dressing to serve with crudités.)

7. If serving the pâté in a bowl or ramekins, you can make a hollow in the centre and fill with some of the fresh tomato dressing, or trickle it over the top with a little extra olive oil. Another suggestion is to spread the pâté thickly on croûtes, sprinkle with freshly grated Parmesan and grill until lightly browned.

⊰ JUDY RODGERS ⊱

BOOK: *The Zuni Café Cookbook*

EVENT MENU: New Year's Eve Gougères with Arugula, Bacon,
and Carol's Pickled Onions, Asparagus and Rice Soup with Pancetta and
Black Pepper, Zuni Roast Chicken with Bread Salad, Mandarins and
Dates Stuffed with Mascarpone, Pomegranates and Pistachios

THANKS TO JUDY RODGERS, the Zuni Café has been a fixture in San Francisco for the past twenty-three years. Having dined there back in the eighties,
I have fond memories of the comfortable room and an approach to food that
blends the casual with cutting-edge cuisine.

So when I discovered that Judy was going to chronicle her culinary journey at Zuni, I encouraged her to fly north and share a bit of her hard-earned
wisdom. I love her book. Every recipe has an abundance of detail. And I en-
courage everyone to read the introduction. You won't find many as inspiring.

But then, this is a woman who is genuinely obsessed with her work. She's
particularly careful to use ingredients produced by farmers who respect the
animals they raise and the earth they plough. Judy is so committed to this
philosophy that she even brought a large bag of tangerines from Michael
Abelman's farm to share with us. Her technique is classically conceived yet
innovative. And there's nothing unexpected about the basic result—a truly
delicious meal.

At the 2003 James Beard Awards, Judy walked away with three prizes—
two for the cookbook and one for best restaurant in the U.S.A.

NEW YEAR'S EVE GOUGÈRES WITH ARUGULA, BACON, AND CAROL'S PICKLED ONIONS

FOR THE BATTER:

1 cup water

3 tablespoons unsalted butter

1 teaspoon salt (a little more if using kosher salt)

4 ounces all-purpose flour (1 cup)

4 large eggs, cold
½ to ¾ teaspoon freshly cracked black pepper
2 ounces Gruyère, cut into ½ inch cubes (about ½ cup)
TO STUFF THE GOUGÈRES:
10 to 12 slices bacon
About 1 ½ ounces arugula, carefully washed and dried
1 cup drained Carol's Pickled Onions (recipe follows)
Makes 20 to 30 three-bite-sized gougères

Preheat the oven to 400°F.

In a 2- to 4-quart saucepan, bring the water, butter, and salt to a simmer over medium heat. Add the flour all at once and stir vigorously until the mixture masses and detaches itself from the sides of the pan. Reduce the heat to low and cook, beating constantly, until the batter is very stiff and almost shiny, usually a few minutes. Off the heat, add the eggs one by one, beating thoroughly with a wooden spoon to completely incorporate each egg before adding the next. The mixture will initially resist each addition; you'll find yourself cutting through and slapping together slabs of slippery, warm paste until it gradually absorbs the egg and becomes sticky again. The final mixture should be no hotter than tepid. Add the pepper to taste and stir in the Gruyère.

If you are proficient with one, transfer the batter to a pastry bag, and pipe 2- to 3-inch-long bands onto a parchment paper–lined (or nonstick) baking sheet about 2 inches apart. Otherwise, use a spoon to scoop out a heaping tablespoon of batter per gougère and a second spoon to scrape it into a peaky mound on the prepared baking sheet.

Bake until firm and a rich golden brown, about 25 minutes. Inevitably, some bits of cheese will ooze and form a delicious, crispy bib on the edges of the gougères. To check doneness, remove 1 gougère and pry open. The interior strands of dough should be tender and moist, but not mushy; if they are, close the gougère and return it to the oven to bake with the rest for another few minutes. If you are concerned they may overbrown, simply turn off the oven and leave to finish cooking in the ambient heat.

Meanwhile, cut the bacon into 1½- to 2-inch segments and panfry or roast to your taste. Drain on towels.

Serve the gougères warm from the oven (or reheated), split through the middle and overstuffed with a few pieces of bacon, several leaves of peppery arugula, and a few ringlets of the pickled onions.

CAROL'S PICKLED ONIONS
12 ounces firm yellow onions,
preferably no more than 2½ inches in diameter
FOR THE BRINE:
1¼ cups Champagne vinegar
or white wine vinegar
1¼ cups water
2 generous tablespoons sugar
2 bay leaves
1 small dried chili
A few whole black peppercorns
Salt
Makes about 1½ pints

Peel and slice the onions into rings about ⅛ inch thick, discarding the end cuts; a mandoline will make this job very easy. The slices will tend to fall into rings on their own, but you may need to separate the tight centers. Discard any green sprouts or pithy or discolored rings.

Combine the vinegar, water, sugar, bay leaves, chili pod, peppercorns, and a few pinches of salt in a small saucepan. If you like things spicy, break the chili pod in half before you add it. Bring to a simmer over medium-low heat, then turn the heat up to medium and add the onion rings. Gently stir the crowded onions as they return to a simmer. Simmer for a little less than 1 minute.

Pour the hot onions and brine into a wide bowl or directly into jars. The skinny rings will turn glassy as they cool. Cover and store refrigerated.

⟞ ℳICHEL ROUX ⟞

BOOK: *New Creative Techniques from a French Master Chef*

EVENT MENU: Tartares of Salmon and Scallops in
Endive Leaves, Terrine of Baby Vegetables, Steamed Fillets of Halibut
in Green Jackets, Leek Coulis with Saffron and Dill,
Rice Pilaf, Poached Pears in Quail's Gate Late Harvest Riesling,
Coffee Sabayon with Cinnamon, Orange Tuiles

I AM EVER GRATEFUL to Whitecap Books for aligning itself with Quadrille
Publishing in England and bringing to town some of our culinary heroes.

Although I'm always pleased to meet a culinary legend such as Michel
Roux, I'm especially happy to observe the enthusiastic response I receive from
our local chefs. Michel's visit allowed me both these pleasures, with a few extra
special moments thrown in for good measure. What a charming man! We held
two events at the shop with Michel, who met and spoke with more than sixty
guests. Each of them was blessed with a little of Michel's magic.

It's quite marvellous to listen to a chef in his sixties whose professional
journey started at the age of fourteen. When that gracious man is standing
before you, generously sharing his experiences, you feel sincerely privileged.

Michel likes this "delicate, flavoursome terrine" served warm or cold
with a pear and lime salsa or a drizzle of olive oil. To warm it, he suggests
you slice the terrine, then steam it for a few minutes.

TERRINE OF BABY VEGETABLES

CELERIAC MOUSSE:

½ celeriac (celery root), about 10 ounces

2 cups heavy cream

4 eggs

3 egg yolks

Salt and freshly ground white pepper

BABY VEGETABLES:

4 ounces baby artichokes

(the kind you can eat raw)

3 tablespoons dry white wine

2 tablespoons olive oil

Juice of 1 lemon

5 ounces baby carrots, peeled

6 ounces baby fennel

6 to 8 medium asparagus spears

4 ounces baby zucchini

4 ounces broccoli florets

4 herb crêpes (see book for details),

11 to 12 inches in diameter

GARNISH:

Confit tomatoes (recipe follows)

Samphire (salicornia or glasswort)

Capers

Fennel fronds

First make the celeriac mousse. Peel the celeriac and cut into 1-inch pieces. Place in a saucepan with the cream and cook gently for about 30 minutes, stirring occasionally, until the celeriac is tender and the cream has reduced by half. Tip into a food processor and whizz for 3 minutes, or until smooth. Leave in the processor to cool slightly, until warm. Add the whole eggs, egg yolks, and seasoning and whizz for 1 minute. Turn into a bowl, cover with plastic wrap, and set aside at room temperature.

To prepare the artichokes, cut off the tips of the leaves with a knife and pare the base to leave only the tender part of the stem and heart. Put the artichokes in a saucepan with the white wine, olive oil, lemon juice, and enough water to cover. Cook over a low heat for about 8 minutes until the artichokes are tender and soft. Allow to cool in the liquid, then drain and pat dry; set aside.

Peel, trim, and wash all the other vegetables. Lightly cook them separately in boiling salted water until *al dente*. Plunge into ice water, drain and pat dry.

Preheat the oven to 325°F. To assemble the terrine, line an 8 × 2½ × 2½-inch narrow loaf pan with plastic wrap, letting it overhang all around.

Use a knife to trim the crêpes into squares and arrange them side-by-side on the plastic wrap, leaving plenty of overhang at both ends and one side of the loaf pan.

Spread a 1¼-inch layer of cold celeriac mousse over the base. Arrange a line of one variety of vegetable over the mousse and cover with more mousse. Gently tap the terrine to settle it and layer the other vegetables and remaining mousse in the same way, finishing with a 1½-inch layer of mousse. Fold the overhanging crêpes, then the plastic wrap over the top. Stand the terrine in a *bain-marie* and cook in the oven for about 1¼ hours. To check if it is cooked, push a trussing needle or fine knife tip into the center for 10 seconds; it should come out clean and feel hot. Let the terrine cool, then refrigerate for at least 24 hours before serving.

To serve, invert the terrine onto a board, unmold and carefully peel off the plastic wrap. Using a fine-bladed knife dipped into warm water, cut into ¾-inch slices. Place on individual plates and garnish with confit tomatoes, some samphire, a few capers, some fennel fronds, and a coarse grinding of white pepper.

CONFIT TOMATOES
2¼ pounds very ripe tomatoes
(preferably plum),
on the stem if possible
1 quart olive oil
2 thyme sprigs
1 bay leaf
2 garlic cloves, peeled and halved
1 teaspoon white peppercorns, crushed
Salt
Makes about 2¼ pounds

Peel the tomatoes, halve or quarter them, and remove the seeds. Heat the oil in a saucepan until very hot but not smoking, then throw in the tomatoes, thyme, bay leaf, garlic, and pepper. Lower the heat and cook gently at about 160°F (barely scalding) for 15 to 20 minutes, depending on how ripe the tomatoes are.

Allow to cool in the pan, then transfer the tomatoes to a jar. Pour in enough oil to cover them, seal the jar with plastic wrap, and refrigerate until needed. Remove the tomatoes from the oil and season with salt to taste just before serving.

⟨ SALLY SCHNEIDER ⟩

BOOK: *A New Way to Cook*

EVENT MENU: Parmesan Crisps, Corn Blini with
Home-Cured Salmon, Fresh Soybeans with Extra-Virgin Olive Oil and
Shaved Cheese, Root Vegetable Crema, Herb-Scented Tuscan
Pork Roast, White Beans and Mellowed Garlic
with Rosemary Oil, Greens with Blood Orange and Hazelnuts,
Mocha Pecan Cake, Apricots Roasted with Cardamom

WHEN YOU HEAR that an author has taken ten years to write a cookbook, you can be relatively certain that the book will be worthwhile. It isn't easy to resist the pressure from colleagues and publishers to rush the book into stores. Putting the reader first takes both confidence and determination. That's why I'm so thankful to Sally Schneider for taking a decade to perfect *A New Way to Cook*.

I'm constantly referring to *A New Way to Cook* for creative ideas and healthy alternatives to traditional favourites. I always follow Sally's advice on not being afraid to improvise. (She was particularly happy when I reported to her that I substituted ground wild boar for the beef in her meatloaf recipe.) I hope it won't be another ten years before Sally returns to Vancouver with her next book. But one thing's for sure: the wait would be worth it.

SALLY WRITES: "Don't worry," Barbara-jo, whom I had never met, said reassuringly over the phone as she figured out ways to help me through a mysterious virus that left me white as a sheet, dizzy and staggeringly exhausted on my arrival to Vancouver. She edited my full schedule down to absolute essentials—willing even to cancel my upcoming event at her store if need be: she made excuses for me and negotiated my dilemma with extraordinary grace.

I was still shaky when I forayed to Barbara-Jo's Books to Cooks to find that Adrienne O'Callaghan had interpreted my recipes so intelligently, deliciously and with such style that my control-freak self had no need to raise her pushy head, even if she'd been able. Kind assistants plied me with tea and found me a cozy place to rest in the back. And when I went to meet the crowd and speak, I found they were so enthusiastic, open and articulate that, for that while, I forgot that I was sick.

The spirit that infused that magic evening took me out of myself, gave me energy I did not have, let me rest in the moment. It did everything I write about good cooking doing: feeding, heartening and transforming body and spirit. Through it, I saw how Barbara-jo generously nourishes our cooking culture—its books and its people. It was like being home.

HERB-SCENTED TUSCAN PORK ROAST

One 7-pound pork loin, boned (have the
butcher do this, reserving the bones), fat trimmed
Tuscan Herb Salt (recipe follows)
Four 10-inch-long rosemary branches
1½ teaspoons kosher salt
3 ounces (4 to 5 thin slices) lean pancetta
1 teaspoon olive oil
2 cups dry white wine
Kosher salt and freshly ground black pepper
Serves 8

Pat the pork loin dry. Using a knife-sharpening steel or a long-handled wooden spoon, pierce a hole lengthwise through the center of the loin. Working from either end of the loin, use your fingers to stuff all but 1 tablespoon of the herb salt into the hole. Insert 1 of the rosemary branches into each end so that it forms a tassle. Mix the remaining herb salt with the 1½ teaspoons salt and rub it all over the roast.

Arrange the pancetta slices, slightly overlapping each other, down the length of the roast. Arrange the 2 remaining rosemary sprigs on top. Tie the roast at 1-inch intervals with cotton string to give it a neat shape (see book for details). Transfer to a platter, cover with plastic wrap, and refrigerate for at least 2 and up to 24 hours. Bring to room temperature for 1 hour before roasting.

Preheat the oven to 450°F.

Place the rack of rib bones curved side down in a shallow roasting pan. Pat the roast dry with paper towels and rub with the olive oil. Place the roast on the rack and roast for 15 minutes. Remove the pan from the oven, turn the roast over, and baste with a few tablespoons of the wine. Return the roast to the oven and reduce the temperature to 350°F. Cook for 1¼ to 1½ hours longer, turning the roast and basting it with wine every 20 minutes; reserve ½ cup of wine for the sauce. The roast is done when an instant-read thermometer inserted in the center registers 145°F.

Transfer the roast to a platter and pour the pan juices into a measuring cup. If the meat on the rack of bones is still pink and you wish to serve the ribs, place on a baking sheet and return to the oven for about 15 minutes.

Meanwhile, place the roasting pan over two burners over moderate heat; when it starts to sizzle, add the reserved ½ cup wine and cook for 2 minutes, scraping up the drippings from the bottom of the pan. Add to the pan juices in the measuring cup; let the fat rise to the surface, about 5 minutes. Skim off the fat and season the sauce with salt and pepper.

Remove the strings and carve the roast into thin slices. If serving the ribs, remove the rack from the pan and cut through the ribs. Arrange the meat and ribs on a platter and serve the pan juices on the side.

TUSCAN HERB SALT

1 garlic clove

1 tablespoon kosher salt

1 small bunch fresh sage (about 30 leaves)

2 sprigs fresh rosemary

Makes about ¼ cup

On a cutting board, mince the garlic with the salt. Place the herbs in a mound and coarsely chop them. Add the garlic and salt and chop them together to make a coarse rub. Use the salt right away, or let it dry, uncovered, in a bowl for a few days.

The dried rub can be stored indefinitely in a clean dry jar.

PEPPERY OR BITTER GREENS WITH SEASONAL FRUITS AND ROASTED NUTS

8 cups (about 12 ounces) trimmed, cleaned,

and dried peppery or bitter greens, such as arugula,

watercress, frisée, Belgian endive, or radicchio

Fruits, such as:

1 medium ripe pear or apple, peeled, cored, and sliced

4 ripe figs, cut into quarters

2 navel or blood oranges, peeled and sectioned

3 mandarin oranges, tangerines,

or clementines, peeled and sectioned

8 kumquats, sliced crosswise into paper-thin slices

SHERRY VINAIGRETTE:

1 teaspoon sherry vinegar

½ teaspoon balsamic vinegar

Pinch of kosher salt

1 tablespoon plus 1 teaspoon extra-virgin olive oil

2 teaspoons water or juice from sectioned citrus fruits

Freshly ground black pepper
2 to 4 tablespoons coarsely chopped roasted nuts,
such as pine nuts, pecans, walnuts, or hazelnuts
Serves 4

1. Put the greens in a large bowl and scatter the fruit over them.
2. In a small bowl or a jar with a lid, combine the sherry vinegar, balsamic vinegar, salt, olive oil, and water. Stir or shake vigorously to emulsify. Drizzle the dressing over the salad and toss to coat, seasoning liberally with pepper.
3. Scatter the nuts over the top. Serve at once.

⤛ FRIEND OF THE SHOP: ⤜
JOHN SCHREINER
John Schreiner is the author of
the British Columbia Wine Companion.

WHEN YOU LIVE in a large city, you're likely to have a plethora of very good food and wine writers. In Vancouver, this is indeed the case. But not many cities have a writer as devoted to his region as John Schreiner. Although the wines of British Columbia have only made an impact on the international scene in recent years, John has penned no less than five books on the subject. His writing has contributed to the growing awareness of our wine industry.

It's a pleasure to host an event with John. He's a gentleman who—though he sensibly totes a backpack and wears galoshes whenever it rains—is always impeccably turned out. His elegant demeanour never fails to remind me of a gentler era. John takes his profession very seriously and dedicates a tremendous amount of time to it. Keep travelling, tasting and writing, Mr. Schreiner.

⊰ ℬONNIE STERN ⊱

BOOK: *HeartSmart Cooking for Family and Friends*
EVENT MENU: Roasted Garlic and Potato Crostini, Sushi Pizza,
Tandoori Salmon, Fragrant Rice with Aromatic Spices,
Raspberry Upside-Down Cake

I FIRST MET BONNIE STERN when she was lured to Vancouver to experience the wonders of our Pacific salmon. I was working at Umberto Menghi's Al Porto restaurant, the host venue for a luncheon that included Bonnie and a number of other prominent Canadian food writers. It was a great coup for me to join this group for the afternoon.

To this day, Bonnie doesn't remember sitting across from me at the table. I barely said a word as I listened to these treasures of the Canadian food scene banter about the great ingredients of our land.

It is very fashionable to converse about such things today, of course. But back then—before the average Canadian had the opportunity to purchase exotic fare in our shops—food writers were strongly encouraged to write recipes that contained readily available and local ingredients. The big difference between then and now is that today our farmers and purveyors produce many of the ingredients we previously imported.

Now when I meet with Bonnie, I am no longer quiet or shy. But she hasn't changed much since we were first introduced: she is still travelling across this vast country and preaching the foodie gospel with the fastest tongue in the Western world.

I don't know anyone who can work more interesting and informative chat into an interview than Bonnie. I love dining with her as she considers how to transform the elegant meal she's eating into a simple recipe that her many fans can enjoy. O Canada, O Bonnie Stern!

ROASTED GARLIC AND POTATO CROSTINI

4 baking potatoes or Yukon Gold potatoes

2 tbsp olive oil

½ tsp salt

¼ tsp pepper

1 tbsp chopped fresh thyme, or pinch dried

1 tbsp chopped fresh rosemary, or pinch dried

ROASTED GARLIC TOPPING:

4 heads garlic

2 oz chèvre (goat cheese), about ½ cup / 125 ml

¼ cup yogurt cheese (see below) or thick yogurt

½ tsp pepper

1 tbsp balsamic vinegar

2 tbsp chopped fresh basil or parsley

1. Slice potatoes into rounds about ½ inch/1 cm thick. Toss with olive oil, salt, pepper, thyme, and rosemary. Arrange in a single layer on baking sheets lined with parchment paper.

2. Cut top quarter off each head of garlic. Wrap garlic in a single layer in foil. Roast garlic and potatoes in a preheated 400°F/200°C oven for 40 to 45 minutes, or until potatoes are brown and crisp and garlic is soft and tender.

3. Squeeze garlic into a food processor or bowl and mash with goat cheese, yogurt cheese, pepper, and vinegar. Stir in basil. Smear some of topping on each potato.

POTATO CROSTINI WITH SMOKED SALMON: Omit garlic topping. Whisk together ½ cup/125 mL yogurt cheese and 1 tsp/5 mL Russian-style mustard. Smear over cooked potatoes. Top with ½ lb/250 g thinly slice smoked salmon, fresh chives, and freshly ground pepper.

YOGURT CHEESE: Line a large strainer with cheesecloth, paper towel or a coffee filter and set over a bowl. Place 3 cups/750 mL unflavoured low-fat natural yogurt in strainer and allow to rest for 3 hours or up to overnight in the refrigerator. About half the volume of yogurt will strain out as liquid (the longer the yogurt sits, the thicker it becomes). Spoon thickened yogurt cheese into a container, cover and refrigerate. Use as required. Makes 1½ cups/375 mL.

≺ *M*ARK STRAUSMAN ≻
BOOK: *The Campagna Table*
EVENT MENU: Summer Tomato Soup, Insalata Caprese,
Penne with Two Sauces: Quick and Fresh Summer Tomato Sauce
and alla Silvana, Tomato Sorbet

MARK STRAUSMAN first came to visit the shop in the autumn of 1999. A devout New Yorker, he was just passing through after a quick trip to Seattle. *The Campagna Table*, a wonderful book named after his New York restaurant, had just been published.

We hosted a small signing in the shop and took Mark on a quick foodie tour to Granville Island via the False Creek ferry. That evening, we ended up at Sun Sui Wah Seafood Restaurant for a feast that included everything from geoduck to chicken feet. No wonder he just had to come back.

Mark came to visit us again the next year. This time, he talked non-stop for two hours while cooking a delicious Italian meal for twenty-six guests. Most times at the shop, we have the meal pretty much prepared for our chef/author guests to assemble, but Mark took on the whole menu and impressed us all.

The tomato season was at its height during Mark's third visit to Vancouver. So we decided to dedicate the menu to this luscious fruit. Milan Djordjevich, the tomato rock star, was kind enough to share his locally grown bounty.

Sadly, Mark's restaurant is gone and *The Campagna Table* is no longer in print. But he's running a great place called Fred's at Barneys New York, the department store on Madison at Sixtieth, and he has joined forces with Pino Luongo at Coco Pazzo (the original) on Seventy-fourth and Madison.

QUICK AND FRESH SUMMER TOMATO SAUCE
1 tablespoon salt, plus additional for seasoning
1 pound fresh or dried pasta, such as spaghetti, penne, or rigatoni
⅓ cup extra-virgin olive oil

1 clove garlic, thickly sliced

12 large ripe tomatoes or 24 ripe plum tomatoes,
coarsely diced, with their juices

1 teaspoon hot red pepper flakes, or to taste

8 fresh basil leaves, torn into small pieces

Makes 6 appetizer servings or 4 main-course servings

In a large covered pot, heat a gallon of water with a tablespoon of salt to a boil. When it boils, add the pasta, stir well, and cover until it returns to the boil. Uncover and boil until just tender to the bite all the way through.

Meanwhile, make the sauce. In a skillet (with a cover) large enough to hold the pasta later on, heat the oil over medium heat. Add the garlic and cook, stirring, until golden. Add the tomatoes, red pepper flakes, and salt to taste, bring to a simmer, and cook about 4 minutes, until the tomatoes are just cooked through. Remove from the heat and stir in the basil.

Reserving ½ cup of the cooking water, drain the pasta in a colander. Add the drained pasta to the sauce and mix well, adding a few tablespoons of pasta cooking water, if needed, to coat the pasta evenly. Cover and cook 1 minute. Taste for salt. Serve immediately.

PENNE ALLA SILVANA

1 tablespoon salt, plus additional for seasoning

¾ pound dried penne

¼ cup extra-virgin olive oil

2 cloves garlic, thickly sliced

One 10-ounce box frozen spinach, thawed and finely chopped

1 cup heavy cream

4 tablespoons butter, cut into pieces

6 tablespoons freshly grated Parmesan cheese

Freshly ground black pepper

Makes 4 appetizer servings

In a large covered pot heat a gallon of water with a tablespoon of salt to a boil. When it boils, add the pasta, stir well, and cover until it returns to the boil. Uncover and boil until just tender to the bite all the way through.

Meanwhile, make the sauce. In a skillet (with a lid) large enough to hold the pasta later on, heat the oil over medium-high heat. Add the garlic and cook, stirring, until golden, about 3 minutes. Add the spinach and mix well. Add the heavy cream, mix, and simmer until slightly thickened.

Reserving ½ cup cooking water, drain the pasta in a colander. Add the drained pasta to the sauce and mix well, adding a few tablespoons of pasta cooking water if needed to coat the pasta evenly. Cover and cook 1 minute. Taste for salt. Mixing with a wooden spoon, add the butter, cheese, and salt and pepper to taste. Serve immediately.

⤝ JOAN TROPIANO TUCCI & ⤞
GIANNI SCAPPIN

BOOK: *Cucina & Famiglia*
EVENT MENU: Timpáno alla Big Night with Ragù Tucci

IF YOU WANT to see me get excited, just mention the name Stanley Tucci.
Since I'm a huge fan of Stanley's movie *Big Night*, I could barely contain my
enthusiasm when publicist Carrie Weinberg called from New York to explain
that Stanley was in Vancouver filming a movie. She was wondering if he
could drop by the store to say hello.

Throughout his life, Stanley has been surrounded by family and friends who share a passion for the pleasures of the table. In fact, Joan Tucci (Stanley's mother) and chef Gianni Scappin (the man who taught Stanley how to cook all those wonderful dishes featured in *Big Night*) had joined forces to write a book about the two things in life that mean everything to them. Hence *Cucina & Famiglia*.

In addition to co-authors Gianni and Joan, Stanley's proud dad—known to one and all as Big Stan—would also be in town to visit Stanley. We didn't have much notice, but everyone at the shop was highly motivated to organize an event. We knew that Stanley might not be able to attend due to his tight shooting schedule, but that didn't stop us from organizing our own Big Night.

The plan was to throw a *timpáno* party. If you've seen *Big Night*, you know what I am talking about. (If you haven't, rent the video now.) After much preparation, our Big Night arrived. We had the soundtrack from the movie playing while the video was silently showing in one corner of the room. Adrienne, with implicit guidance from the Tucci elders, prepared a fabulous *timpáno*. We ate, we drank, we laughed, we cried. Stanley wasn't able to attend our celebration, but his spirit was definitely there. I'll always remember it as one of the shop's truly magical evenings.

TIMPÁNO ALLA BIG NIGHT

Note: You will need an 8-quart
casserole dish for this dish.

FOR THE DOUGH:

4 cups all-purpose flour

4 large eggs

1 teaspoon kosher salt

3 tablespoons olive oil

½ cup water

TO PREPARE THE PAN:

Butter

Olive oil

FOR THE FILLING:

2 cups ¼ × ½-inch Genoa salami pieces

2 cups ¼ × ½-inch sharp provolone cheese cubes

12 hard-boiled eggs, shelled,

quartered lengthwise,

and each quarter cut in half

to create chunks

2 cups little meatballs (recipe follows)

8 cups Ragù Tucci (recipe follows)

3 pounds ziti, cooked very *al dente*

(about half the time recommended on the package)

and drained (18 cups cooked)

2 tablespoons olive oil

⅔ cup finely grated pecorino Romano cheese

4 large eggs, beaten

To make the dough, place the flour, eggs, salt, and olive oil in a stand mixer fitted with the dough hook. (A large-capacity food processor may also be used.) Add 3 tablespoons of the water and process. Add more water, 1 tablespoon at time, until the mixture comes together and forms a ball. Turn the dough out onto a lightly floured work surface and knead to make sure it is well mixed. Set aside to rest for 5 minutes.

(To knead the dough by hand, mix the flour and salt together on a clean, dry work surface or pastry board. Form these dry ingredients into a mound and then make a well in the center. Break the eggs into the center of the well and lightly beat them with a fork. Stir in 3 tablespoons of the water. Use the fork to gradually incorporate some of the dry ingredients into the egg mixture. Continue mixing the dry ingredients into the eggs, adding the remaining water 1 tablespoon at a time. Knead the dough with your hands to make a well-mixed, smooth, dry dough. If the dough becomes too sticky, add more flour. Set aside to rest for 5 minutes).

Flatten the dough out on a lightly floured work surface. Dust the top of the dough with flour and roll it out, dusting with flour and flipping the dough over from time to time, until it is about ¹⁄₁₆ inch thick and is the desired diameter.

Generously grease the *timpáno* baking pan with butter and olive oil. Fold the dough in half and then in half again, to form a triangle, and place it in the pan. Open the dough and arrange it in the pan, gently pressing it against the bottom and the sides, draping the extra dough over the sides. Set aside.

Preheat the oven to 350° F.

To prepare the filling, have the salami, provolone, hard-boiled eggs, meatballs and ragù at room temperature. Toss the drained pasta with the olive oil and 2 cups of the ragù. Distribute 6 generous cups of the pasta on the bottom of the *timpáno*. Top with 1 cup of the salami, 1 cup of the provolone, 6 of the hard-boiled eggs, 1 cup of the meatballs, and ⅓ cup of the Romano cheese. Pour 2 cups of the ragù over these ingredients. Top with 6 cups of the remaining pasta. Top that with the remaining 1 cup salami, 1 cup provolone, 6 hard-boiled eggs, 1 cup meatballs, and ⅓ cup Romano cheese. Pour 2 cups of the ragù over these ingredients. Top with the remaining 6 cups pasta. (The ingredients should now be about 1 inch below the rim of the pot) Spoon the remaining 2 cups ragù over the pasta. Pour the beaten eggs over the filling. Fold the pasta dough over the filling to seal completely. Trim away and discard any double layers of dough.

Bake until lightly browned, about 1 hour. Then cover with aluminum foil and continue baking until the *timpáno* is cooked through and the dough is golden brown (and reaches and internal temperature of 120 degrees F), about 30 minutes. Remove from the oven and allow to rest for 30 or more minutes. The baked *timpáno* should not adhere to the pan. If any part is still attached, carefully detach with a knife. Grasp the baking pan firmly and invert the *timpáno* onto a serving platter. Remove the pan and allow the *timpáno* to cool for 20 minutes. Using a long, sharp knife, cut a circle about 3 inches in diameter in the center of the *timpáno*, making sure to cut all the way through to the bottom. Then slice the *timpáno* as you would a pie into individual portions, leaving the center circle as a support for the remaining pieces.

RAGÙ TUCCI

(Meat-Based Tomato Sauce Tucci-Style)

Note: When preparing ragù for *timpáno,* only the sauce is used
and the meat is served as a separate course. The sauce for *timpáno* should
be thin, so measure out 7½ cups of prepared sauce and
stir in ½ cup water before proceeding with the *timpáno* recipe.

¼ cup olive oil

1 pound stewing beef, trimmed of fat, rinsed,
patted dry, and cut into pieces

1 pound country-style spareribs, trimmed of fat,
cut in half, rinsed, and patted dry

1 cup roughly chopped onions

3 cloves garlic, roughly chopped

½ cup dry red wine

One 6-ounce can tomato paste

1½ cups warm water

8 cups canned whole plum tomatoes (about two 35-ounce cans),
passed through a food mill or pureed in the blender

3 fresh basil leaves

1 tablespoon chopped fresh oregano leaves or 1 teaspoon dried

Makes 8 servings

Warm the oil in a stew pot set over medium-high heat. Sear the stewing beef
until brown on all sides, about 10 minutes. Remove from the pot and set aside
in a bowl. Add the spareribs to the pot and sear until they are brown on all
sides, about 10 minutes. Remove the ribs and set aside in the bowl with the
stewing beef. (If your pot is big enough to hold all of the meat in a single
layer, it may be cooked at the same time.)

Stir the onions and garlic into the pot. Reduce the heat to low and cook
until the onions begin to soften and lose their shape, about 5 minutes. Stir
in the wine, scraping the bottom of the pot clean. Add the tomato paste. Pour
½ cup of the warm water into the can to loosen any residual paste and then

pour the water into the pot. Cook to warm the paste through, about 2 minutes. Add the tomatoes along with the remaining 1 cup warm water. Stir in the basil and oregano. Cover with the lid slightly askew and simmer to sweeten the tomatoes, about 30 minutes.

Return the meat to the pot, along with any juices that have accumulated in the bowl. Cover with the lid slightly askew and simmer, stirring frequently, until the meat is very tender and the tomatoes are cooked, about 2 hours. Warm water may be added to the sauce, in ½-cup portions, if the sauce becomes too thick. (If you have made meatballs, they may be added during the last half hour of cooking. The meatballs will soften and absorb some of the sauce.)

POLPETTE
(Meatballs)

Ten 1-inch-thick slices Italian bread
1 pound ground beef chuck
2 tablespoons chopped fresh parsley leaves
2 cloves garlic, finely chopped
1 large egg
5 tablespoons finely grated pecorino Romano cheese
Kosher salt and freshly ground pepper
2 tablespoons olive oil

Arrange the bread on a cookie sheet and allow it to dry out, uncovered, about 3 days. Place the dried bread in a bowl and cover with warm water. Set aside until the bread softens, about 5 minutes.

In another bowl, combine the meat, parsley, garlic, egg, cheese, and salt and pepper to taste, using your hands to mix the ingredients. Remove and discard the crust from each slice of bread. Squeeze the water out of the bread, and breaking it into small pieces, add it to the meat. Work the bread into the meat until they are equally combined and the mixture holds together like a soft dough.

Warm the olive oil in a large frying pan set over medium-high heat. Scoop out a heaping tablespoon of the meat mixture. Roll it between the plams of your hands to form a ball about 1½ inches in diameter. (Meatballs that are being prepared for *timpáno* should be very small. Use a ½ teaspoon to scoop out the dough and form it into ½-inch balls.) Cook one meatball until well browned on all sides, about 8 minutes. (A meatball that sticks to the pan is not ready to be turned.) Taste the meatball, and if needed, adjust the seasoning of the remaining mixture by adding more cheese or salt and pepper. Proceed to cook the meatballs in small batches. As each batch is completed, remove it to a warm serving plate. Serve when all the meatballs are cooked.

*D*AVID VELJACIC

BOOK: *The Fire Chef*

EVENT MENU: Piquant Pineapple Slices, Buttered Portobello Mushrooms, Mini Hamburgers, Barbecued Country Style Spare Ribs, Dalmatian Barbecue Squid stuffed with Shrimp and Garlic

I CAN APPRECIATE a sultry summer evening as well as anyone, but the first and only time David Veljacic came to visit left me with the warmest of memories. David pulled up in front of the shop with his truck, towing a barbecue on wheels. He felt it was best to do his show right there on the street. The smoke was billowing and the smells of barbecue wafted through the neighbourhood. The men were thrilled, but all this fiery activity on the street made me nervous. Ultimately, I decided not to worry. The Fire Chef—with all the necessary credentials—was here.

Sadly, David did not make it back to the shop for a second visit.

Food and wine writer and broadcaster Jurgen Gothe remembers the Fire Chef:

So *The Fire Chef*, David Veljacic's first book, landed on my desk and at a glance I wasn't much impressed. Another boring book about barbecuing, I figured; worse, a barbecue book from a publisher known more for worthy, grant-reliant tomes than for books about everyday cooking.

But something drew me in—maybe the succulent slab o' meat on the cover, with black-eyed peas and peppers on the side. As an unrepentant carnivore, that sort of thing gets me excited. I opened the book at random, to page 14, and there it was: "How to Grill the Perfect Steak." I could *use* this information, having long been barbecue-challenged. Maybe this would be the book to change all that. Suddenly zipping through my mind's VCR were memories of hundreds, thousands of dollars wasted turning perfectly fine meat into charcoal.

"Buy 6-ounce filets mignons 1 inch thick," began the mantra I committed to memory soon after the first filet came off the grill. David was right. The drill was right. The steaks were right. I gave the recipe on the air one afternoon and got a lot of argument from listeners. They were all wrong. David was right.

And he continued to be right with other food in the book. Many of his recipes have become staples in my limited repertoire of solid favourites. The succulent prime rib (page 48), the pork tenderloin with mustard, lemon and rosemary (page 112), the *čevapčiči* (Croatian grilled lamb and veal sausages) with red onion and sweet mustard (page 121) and a dozen more dishes came home to dazzle the diners—friends and family—to say nothing of the dog.

The Fire Chef became my culinary messiah and I his prophet. I reviewed the book in every venue available to me—on radio, public and private; in print, newsy and glossy-foodie; on television and in live appearances. I bought a couple dozen copies and gave them as gifts. I proselytized endlessly: "Can you believe it? Before this book I couldn't barbecue a damn thing and now I'm saved!" Zeal, especially when flavoured with David's salt-free barbecue rub, is wonderfully energizing.

David tracked me down and called to say, "Hey, how come you're giving me all this publicity?" "Because you rock, Fire Chef," I said, "this stuff *works!*" We would talk on the phone a number of times after that, but I only met David once. It was the week of Christmas the following year and I was alone in a cavernous office near Vancouver City Hall. Early one afternoon someone stepped out of the elevator that opened directly into the office. I heard steps, a rustle of paper, one of those tentative "Is anybody there?" coughs and a voice venturing hello.

The Fire Chef had come calling, carrying a goodie bag. "Brought you some stuff," he muttered, and out tumbled mason jars and shakers and Ziploc bags of Mexican oregano powder and Pappy's Salt-Free Seasoning, Tellicherry black pepper, onion granules and lemon powder. "I bring the stuff in, from Texas," he continued. "Thanks for everything. Merry Christmas." We shook hands and that was it: the first time we met, and the last.

The herbs and spices became the *schatzkammer* of my kitchen. Immediately I made up batches of my favourite dry rubs and marinades. The meats tasted even better. The Christmas gift dilemma had been effectively solved. And so it went.

One day I got word that the Fire Chef was ailing. And then came a call from Barbara-jo McIntosh. She had organized a cook 'n' read, meet 'n' eat session with David at her marvellous Yaletown store. David was too ill to come. Would I stand in?

I can't recall having been more pleased and more proud to go to a book-anything than I was to go to that one. What's more, I didn't have to cook—it's one of a handful of things I won't do in public, with people watching. Just kind of a quirk. No, the amazing and adept Adrienne O'Callaghan did it all—she prepared mini burgers and chicken sections and sundry seared meats, and she made salsas, all out of the book that had become my bible. And all made on a regulation-issue Canadian Tire barbecue chained to a parking meter outside the store.

The guests came, the wine was poured, the food went 'round, and I got to mingle with the guests and talk. I shared anecdotes, observations, food reminiscences, but mostly I said my litany: Before I met David Veljacic I couldn't barbecue worth a damn. Now I'm saved. Hallelujah.

Along with *The Joy of Cooking*, some M.F.K. Fisher, a well-thumbed Theodora FitzGibbon, Jack Denton Scott's pasta cookery book, and one or two other books, *The Fire Chef* is in my carry-on for the overnight flight to the hereafter. I don't expect David in the arrivals lounge but I'll run into him sooner or later, somewhere, standing in front of a barbecue. "Hey," I'll say, "I brought you some stuff." And out of the bag will come a magnum of Petrus, some decent late-eighties vintage, and we'll pull the cork, inhale the aroma and drink it right out of the bottle. Then, he'll barbecue us some meat.

And that's what heaven's all about, I figure.

DALMATIAN BARBECUE SQUID
STUFFED WITH SHRIMP AND GARLIC

20 small squid bodies, cleaned
and with the outer membrane left on
¼ lb shrimp meat, minced fine
3 tbsp fine bread crumbs
2 tbsp green onions, minced fine
1 tbsp olive oil
½ tbsp black pepper
¼ cup olive oil
4 garlic cloves, minced fine
3 tbsp fresh parsley, minced

Serves 4

Combine the shrimp meat, bread crumbs, green onions, 1 tablespoon of olive oil and the black pepper in a bowl.

Stuff equal amounts of the shrimp mixture loosely into each squid body. Do not overstuff as squid have a high water content which makes them shrink when cooked. If they are overstuffed, they will split open. When the squid are stuffed, cook immediately or refrigerate until ready for use.

Prepare a basting sauce by combining the olive oil, garlic and parsley in a bowl.

Grill the squid over a low to medium heat (250 to 350°F) for approximately 15 minutes. Roll them up and down the grid to cook all over. Baste with the sauce often. Turn the heat to high and grill the squid until they are slightly charred on all sides.

Make a slight slit, lengthwise, on the squid. Baste any remaining sauce into the slits. Turn the heat off, close the lid and allow to sit for 2 minutes before serving.

⊰ *P*ATRICIA WELLS ⊱

BOOK: *The Paris Cookbook*
EVENT MENU: Taillevent Goat Cheese and Dried Tomato Appetizer,
Toasty Salted Almonds, JR's Parmesan Chips, Tapenade,
Boulevard Raspail Cream of Mushroom Soup, Les Allobroges's
Braised Lamb Shanks with Garlic, Benoît's Carrots
with Cumin and Orange, Honey Rosemary-Ginger Ice Cream, Carré
des Feuillants's Honey-Poached Pears in Beaumes-de-Venise

THE STORY IS a sweet one. The husband is transferred to Paris to work for the *Herald Tribune*. The wife cooks, eats and visits all the great cafés in this magnificent city. The wife is hired to write a column critiquing restaurants for her husband's paper. The couple acquires a country home in Provence, and the wife opens a cooking school. The husband quits work. They came for him and stayed for her. I love it.

On top of everything else, Patricia Wells writes wonderful cookbooks. Joël Robuchon, one of the great chefs of France, co-authored an earlier publication with her—and that gives a girl real power.

But what really impressed me about Madame? She was in Vancouver for two days, and I wanted to split her media duties over the forty-eight hours. Patricia, however, wanted to spend Sunday with friends and work on Monday.

Here's how her day went. On Monday morning, she rose early to work out. At 8:45 AM, she was picked up and driven to her first radio interview. From there she left to tape a TV segment with Nathan Fong. Then it was off to CTV to tape a guest spot with Vicki Gabereau. After that, I picked her up and took her to lunch with *The Vancouver Sun*'s Murray McMillan. Then she was interviewed by CBC French radio and *The Georgia Straight*'s Angela Murrills. Following an amazing event at Le Crocodile, Patricia taught a class at the shop. After that, she really wanted to go to Tojo's for dinner. On Tuesday morning, she was off to New York. But not before working out. Are you tired yet?

LES ALLOBROGES'S
BRAISED LAMB SHANKS WITH GARLIC

4 teaspoons Quatre Epices (recipe follows)

4 meaty lamb shanks (each about a pound;
do not trim the external fat)

Sea salt to taste

Freshly ground white pepper to taste

1 cup Banyuls wine, *vin doux naturel* from Provence, or Port

1 quart Homemade Chicken Stock
(see book for details)

1 recipe Garlic Confit (recipe follows)

4 servings

1. Preheat oven to 450 degrees F.

2. Rub Quatre Epices over the surface of the lamb shanks. Season them with sea salt and white pepper.

3. Stand the shanks, wider side down, narrow end up, in a large roasting pan. Place the pan in the center of the oven and roast, uncovered, for 1 hour.

4. Transfer the lamb to a platter and set aside. Off the heat, deglaze the pan with the wine, scraping up any cooked bits that may have stuck to the bottom. Return the lamb to the pan standing on end, wider side down. Add the stock. Cover the pan and return it to the oven. Braise, without disturbing the meat, until the meat is very tender and just beginning to fall off the bone, about 1½ hours.

5. Remove the pan from the oven and transfer the lamb shanks to a warm platter. Cover them with foil and let them rest for 10 minutes. Meanwhile, strain the sauce through a fine-mesh sieve into a gravy boat. Serve, passing the sauce and the Garlic Confit.

QUATRE EPICES

(Four-spice blend)

1 teaspoon allspice berries

1 teaspoon whole cloves

1 teaspoon freshly ground nutmeg

1 teaspoon cinnamon

One by one, grind the allspice and cloves in a spice grinder. Combine the spices in a small bowl, add the freshly grated nutmeg and ground cinnamon, and use immediately.

LES ALLOBROGES'S GARLIC CONFIT

(*Confit d'ail les allobroges*)

4 plump, fresh heads garlic,

separated into cloves but not peeled

1 cup extra-virgin olive oil

Makes 1 ½ cups

Place the garlic in a small saucepan, and cover with the oil. Cook, uncovered, at the barest simmer over the lowest possible heat until the garlic is soft and a small knife inserted into a clove meets no resistance, 45 minutes to 1 hour. (Watch carefully to avoid burning the garlic. You may need to place the saucepan on a flame tamer.) The garlic can be served immediately or allowed to cool in the oil. Reheat at serving time. Allow guests to pop the cloves of garlic out of their skins. The oil can be used in cooking or for preparing a vinaigrette.

≺ $\mathcal{M}$ARTIN YAN ≻

BOOK: *Martin Yan's Chinatown Cooking*
EVENT MENU: Market Basket Vegetable Stir-Fry

A FEW YEARS AGO, Martin Yan wrote a book called *Chinese Cooking for Dummies.* I was told he could come to Vancouver for a very short visit. He flew into Vancouver, was whisked to the shop and took a few moments to organize himself (and us). He then proceeded to entertain thirty enthusiastic guests who stood around the counter while Master Yan chopped with the speed of light. Forty-five minutes later, he was on his way back to the airport.

I must admit that I thought Martin was a tad grumpy. Of course, I was entertained by his skill and amused by his antics. But we didn't really

connect. So when the publisher called to request an event with Martin for his Chinatown book, I said yes with some reserve. Fortunately, Martin's second visit worked out beautifully.

I felt it most appropriate that Martin take a group of guests on a tour of our Chinatown, as it is featured in the book. On a beautiful Saturday morning the group met at Dr. Sun Yat-Sen Classical Chinese Garden, and the tour began. I walk through Chinatown frequently, but with Martin the journey was nothing short of amazing. Shoppers and vendors alike were delighted to have this culinary star in their neighbourhood. We purchased some choice ingredients and went back to the shop where—once again—we were wowed by Martin's skills in the kitchen. Come back anytime you wish, Master Yan.

MARKET BASKET VEGETABLE STIR-FRY

(Don't be limited by the ingredient list;
substitute your favorite vegetables.)

3 dried black mushrooms

4 dried wood ear mushrooms

1 piece dried snow fungus (optional)

FOR THE SEASONINGS

2 tablespoons oyster-flavored sauce

1 tablespoon soy sauce

2 teaspoons sesame oil

2 tablespoons vegetable oil

2 garlic cloves, minced

1 cup broccoli florets

1 cup cauliflower florets

½ cup diced (1-inch squares) purple cabbage

½ cup Vegetable Stock or canned vegetable broth

1 cup snow peas, trimmed

½ cup bean sprouts

Serves 4 as part of a multicourse meal

1. Put the black mushrooms, wood ears, and snow fungus in separate small bowls and pour enough warm water over them to cover. Soak until softened, about 20 minutes. Drain. Discard the black mushroom stems and cut the caps in half. Thinly slice the wood ears. Discard the hard yellow portion of the snow fungus, then cut the remainder into bite-sized pieces.

2. Prepare the seasonings: Stir the oyster-flavored sauce, soy sauce, and sesame oil together in a small bowl.

3. Heat a wok over high heat until hot. Add the oil and swirl to coat the sides. Add the garlic and stir-fry until fragrant, about 20 seconds. Add the broccoli, cauliflower, cabbage, vegetable stock, black mushrooms, wood ears, and snow fungus, cover the wok, and cook until the cauliflower is tender-crisp, 2 to 2½ minutes.

4. Add the seasonings, snow peas, and sprouts and stir-fry until the snow peas are tender, about 1 minute. Scoop onto a serving platter and serve.

COOKS WHO SHOULD
HAVE BOOKS

I MENTIONED in my introduction that the success of the events at the shop has been enhanced by many local chefs, restaurateurs and purveyors who do not have books. But I predict that soon many of them will.

Douglas Anderson, Scott Baechler, Jean-Yves Benoit, John Blakely, Michael Brough, Chris Brown, Rob Clark, Sean Cousins, Brad Ellis, Nathan Fong, Peter Fong, Michelle Geris, Thomas Haas, David Hawksworth, Gennaro Iorio, Michel Jacob, Scott Jaeger, Assefa Kebede, Lynda Larouche, Don Letendre, Bruno Marti, Michael Noble, Adrienne O'Callaghan, Nobu Ochi, Frank Pabst, Harry and Thea Prinianakis, Pino Posteraro, Romy Prasad, Alessandra and Jean-Francis Quaglia, Montri Rattanaraj, Fabrice Rossman, Alice and Alison Spurrell, Hidekazo Tojo, Edward Tuson, Vikram and Meeru Vij, James Walt . . .

PERMISSSIONS

"Aromatic Lemongrass Patties" and "Yunnan Greens" extracted from *Hot Sour Salty Sweet* by Jeffrey Alford and Naomi Duguid. Copyright © by Jeffrey Alford and Naomi Duguid. Reprinted by permission of Random House Canada. "Tiramisu" from *Saveur Cooks Authentic Italian*. Copyright © by Saveur (World Publications). Reprinted by permission of the author and World Publications. "Simply the Best Scalloped Potatoes" extracted from *The Complete Canadian Living Cookbook* by Elizabeth Baird and the Canadian Living Test Kitchen. Copyright © 2001 by Transcontinental Media Inc. Reprinted by permission of Random House Canada. "Pesto Crusted Halibut with Red Lentil Dahl" from *Simply Bishop's* by John Bishop and Dennis Green. Copyright © 2002 by John Bishop. Reprinted by permission of the authors and Douglas & McIntyre. "Pasta alla Gricia" and "Fastest Roast Chicken" from *The Minimalist Cooks Dinner* by Mark Bittman, published by Random House, Broadway Books. Copyright © 2001 by Mark Bittman. Reprinted by permission of the author. "(I Can't Believe It's Not) Creamed Corn" from *Off the Eaten Path* by Bob Blumer, published by Ballantine Books. Copyright © 2000 by Bob Blumer. Reprinted by permission of the author. "Brandied Eggnog Cookies" from *The Good Cookie* by Tish Boyle, published by John Wiley & Sons. Copyright © 2002 by Tish Boyle. Reprinted by permission of the author. "Flaming Spinach Salad" from *Zest for Life* by Diane Clement, published in 2000 by Raincoast Books. Reprinted by permission of the publisher. "Toasted Hazelnut Pound Cake" extracted from *In the Sweet Kitchen* by Regan Daley. Copyright © 2000 by Regan Daley. Reprinted by permission of Random House Canada. "Smokey Eggplant Dip, Seed Bread" from *Tom Douglas's Seattle Kitchen* by Tom Douglas. Copyright © 2001 by Tom Douglas. Reprinted by permission of HarperCollins Publishers Inc., William Morrow. "Little Egg and Ham Pies" from *Simple Food* by Jill Dupleix. Copyright © by Jill Dupleix. Reprinted by permission of Quadrille Publishing Limited. "Tuna Tartare with Tamari Vinaigrette" from *Rob Feenie Cooks at Lumière* by Rob

RECIPE INDEX